W9-CAV-769

2nd EDITION

Ventures 2

STUDENT'S BOOK

Gretchen Bitterlin   Dennis Johnson   Donna Price   Sylvia Ramirez

K. Lynn Savage (Series Editor)

CAMBRIDGE
UNIVERSITY PRESS

CAMBRIDGE
UNIVERSITY PRESS

University Printing House, Cambridge CB2 8BS, United Kingdom

One Liberty Plaza, 20th Floor, New York, NY 10006, USA

477 Williamstown Road, Port Melbourne, VIC 3207, Australia

4843/24, 2nd Floor, Ansari Road, Daryaganj, Delhi – 110002, India

79 Anson Road, #06–04/06, Singapore 079906

Cambridge University Press is part of the University of Cambridge.

It furthers the University's mission by disseminating knowledge in the pursuit of education, learning and research at the highest international levels of excellence.

www.cambridge.org
Information on this title: www.cambridge.org/9781107687226

© Cambridge University Press 2014

This publication is in copyright. Subject to statutory exception and to the provisions of relevant collective licensing agreements, no reproduction of any part may take place without the written permission of Cambridge University Press.

First published 2008
20 19 18 17 16 15 14 13 12

Printed in Dubai by Oriental Press

A catalogue record for this publication is available from the British Library

ISBN 978-1-107-68722-6 Student's Book with Audio CD
ISBN 978-1-107-63538-8 Workbook with Audio CD
ISBN 978-1-139-87102-0 Online Workbook
ISBN 978-1-107-66579-8 Teacher's Edition with Audio CD / CD-ROM
ISBN 978-1-107-66009-0 Class Audio CDs
ISBN 978-1-107-67928-3 Presentation Plus

Additional resources for this publication at www.cambridge.org/ventures

Cambridge University Press has no responsibility for the persistence or accuracy of URLs for external or third-party internet websites referred to in this publication, and does not guarantee that any content on such websites is, or will remain, accurate or appropriate.

Art direction, book design, photo research, and layout services: Q2A / Bill Smith
Audio production: CityVox, LLC

Authors' acknowledgments

The authors would like to acknowledge and thank focus group participants and reviewers for their insightful comments, as well as Cambridge University Press editorial, marketing, and production staffs, whose thorough research and attention to detail have resulted in a quality product.

The publishers would also like to extend their particular thanks to the following reviewers and consultants for their valuable insights and suggestions:

Kit Bell, LAUSD division of Adult and Career Education, Los Angeles, CA; **Bethany Bogage**, San Diego Community College District, San Diego, CA; **Leslie Keaton Boyd**, Dallas ISD, Dallas, TX; **Barbara Brodsky**, Teaching Work Readiness English for Refugees – Lutheran Family Services, Omaha, NE; **Jessica Buchsbaum**, City College of San Francisco, San Francisco, CA; **Helen Butner**, University of the Fraser Valley, British Columbia, Canada; **Sharon Churchill Roe**, Acadia University, Wolfville, NS, Canada; **Lisa Dolehide**, San Mateo Adult School, San Mateo, CA; **Yadira M. Dominguez**, Dallas ISD, Dallas, TX; **Donna M. Douglas**, College of DuPage, Glen Ellyn, IL; **Latarsha Dykes**, Broward Collge, Pembroke Pines, FL; **Megan L. Ernst**, Glendale Community College, Glendale, CA; **Megan Esler**, Portland Community College, Portland, OR; **Jennifer Fadden**, Fairfax County Public Schools, Fairfax, VA; **Fotine Fahouris**, College of Marin, Kentfield, CA; **Lynn Francis**, M.A, M.S., San Diego Community College, San Diego, CA; **Danielle Gines**, Tarrant County College, Arlington, TX; **Katherine Hayne**, College of Marin, Kentfield, CA; **Armenuhi Hovhannes**, City College of San Francisco, San Francisco, CA; **Fayne B. Johnson**; **Martha L. Koranda**, College of DuPage, Glen Ellyn, IL; **Daphne Lagios**, San Mateo Adult School, San Mateo, CA; **Judy Langelier**, School District of Palm Beach County, Wellington, FL; **Janet Les**, Chilliwack Community Services, Chilliwack, British Columbia, Canada; **Keila Louzada**, Northern Virginia Community College, Sterling, VA; **Karen Mauer**, Fort Worth ISD, Fort Worth, TX; **Silvana Mehner**, Northern Virginia Community College, Sterling, VA; **Astrid T. Mendez-Gines,** Tarrant County College, Arlington, TX; **Beverly A. Miller**, Houston Community College, Houston, TX; **José Montes, MS. Ed.**, The English Center, Miami-Dade County Public Schools, Miami, FL; **Suzi Monti**, Community College of Baltimore County, Baltimore, MD; **Irina Morgunova**, Roxbury Community College, Roxbury Crossing, MA; **Julia Morgunova**, Roxbury Community College, Roxbury Crossing, MA; **Susan Otero**, Fairfax County Public Schools, Fairfax, VA; **Sergei Paromchik**, Hillsborough County Public Schools, Tampa, FL; **Pearl W. Pigott**, Houston Community College, Houston, TX; **Marlene Ramirez**, The English Center, Miami-Dade County Public Schools, Miami, FL; **Cory Rayala**, Harbor Service Center, LAUSD, Los Angeles, CA; **Catherine M. Rifkin**, Florida State College at Jacksonville, Jacksonville, FL; **Danette Roe**, Evans Community Adult School, Los Angeles, CA; **Maria Roy**, Kilgore College, Kilgore, TX; **Jill Shalongo**, Glendale Community College, Glendale, CA, and Sierra Linda High School, Phoenix, AZ; **Laurel Owensby Slater**, San Diego Community College District, San Diego, CA; **Rheba Smith**, San Diego Community College District, San Diego, CA; **Jennifer Snyder**, Portland Community College, Portland, OR; **Mary K. Solberg**, Metropolitan Community College, Omaha, NE; **Rosanne Vitola**, Austin Community College, Austin, TX

Scope and sequence

UNIT TITLE TOPIC	FUNCTIONS	LISTENING AND SPEAKING	VOCABULARY	GRAMMAR FOCUS
Welcome pages 2–5	▪ Describing skills ▪ Giving personal information	▪ Talking about what classmates can do ▪ Asking and answering questions about personal information	▪ Review of regular and irregular verbs	▪ Review of *be* – present and past ▪ Review of present and past of regular and irregular verbs
Unit 1 **Personal information** pages 6–17 Topic: **Describing people**	▪ Describing height, hair, and eyes ▪ Describing clothing ▪ Describing habitual actions ▪ Describing actions in the present	▪ Describing what people look like ▪ Asking and describing what people are wearing ▪ Asking and describing what people are doing at the present time ▪ Asking and describing people's habitual actions	▪ Accessories ▪ Adjectives of size, color, and pattern	▪ Adjective order ▪ Present continuous vs. simple present ▪ *and… too*, *and… either*, and *but*
Unit 2 **At school** pages 18–29 Topic: **School services**	▪ Offering advice ▪ Describing wants ▪ Describing future plans	▪ Asking and describing what people want and need ▪ Asking about and describing future plans	▪ Computer terms ▪ Vocational courses	▪ *Want* and *need* ▪ The future with *will*, *be going to*, and the present continuous
Review: Units 1 and 2 pages 30–31		▪ Understanding a narrative		
Unit 3 **Friends and family** pages 32–43 Topic: **Friends**	▪ Describing past actions ▪ Describing daily activities	▪ Asking and answering questions about past actions ▪ Asking and answering questions about daily habits	▪ Parts of a car ▪ Daily activities	▪ Review of simple past with regular and irregular verbs ▪ Simple present vs. simple past ▪ Collocations with *make* and *do*; *play* and *go*
Unit 4 **Health** pages 44–55 Topic: **Accidents**	▪ Identifying appropriate action after an accident ▪ Asking for and giving advice ▪ Expressing necessity ▪ Showing understanding	▪ Asking for and giving advice ▪ Clarifying meaning	▪ Health problems ▪ Accidents ▪ Terms on medicine packaging	▪ *Should* ▪ *Have to* + verb ▪ *Must*, *must not*, *have to*, *not have to*
Review: Units 3 and 4 pages 56–57		▪ Understanding a narrative		
Unit 5 **Around town** pages 58–69 Topic: **Transportation**	▪ Identifying methods of transportation ▪ Describing number of times ▪ Describing length of time	▪ Asking and answering questions about train, bus, and airline schedules ▪ Asking and answering questions about personal transportation habits ▪ Describing personal habits	▪ Train station terms ▪ Travel activities ▪ Adverbs of frequency	▪ *How often* and *How long* questions ▪ Adverbs of frequency ▪ Prepositions (*into*, *out of*, *through*, and *toward*)

READING	WRITING	LIFE SKILLS	PRONUNCIATION
■ Reading a story about someone's family	■ Writing verb forms in past and present	■ Talking about your skills	■ Pronouncing key vocabulary
■ Reading an e-mail about a family member ■ Scanning to find the answers to questions	■ Writing a descriptive paragraph about a classmate ■ Using a comma after time phrases at the beginning of a sentence	■ Reading an order form	■ Pronouncing key vocabulary
■ Reading a short essay on an application form ■ Skimming for the main idea	■ Writing an expository paragraph about goals ■ Using *First*, *Second*, and *Third* to organize ideas	■ Reading course descriptions ■ Setting short-term goals	■ Pronouncing key vocabulary
			■ Recognizing and pronouncing strong syllables
■ Reading a personal journal entry ■ Scanning for *First*, *Next*, and *Finally* to order events	■ Writing a personal journal entry about the events of a day ■ Using a comma after sequence words	■ Reading a cell phone calling-plan brochure	■ Pronouncing key vocabulary
■ Reading a warning label ■ Understanding a bulleted list	■ Filling out an accident report form ■ Using cursive writing for a signature	■ Reading medicine labels ■ Understanding a warning label	■ Pronouncing key vocabulary
			■ Recognizing and emphasizing important words
■ Reading a personal letter ■ Scanning for capital letters to determine names of cities and places	■ Writing a personal letter about a trip ■ Spelling out hours and minutes from one to ten in writing	■ Reading a bus schedule ■ Reading a train schedule ■ Reading an airline schedule	■ Pronouncing key vocabulary

UNIT TITLE TOPIC	FUNCTIONS	LISTENING AND SPEAKING	VOCABULARY	GRAMMAR FOCUS
Unit 6 **Time** pages 70–81 Topic: **Time lines and major events**	■ Describing major events in the past ■ Inquiring about life events	■ Asking and answering questions about major life events in the past ■ Ordering events in the past	■ Life events ■ Time phrases	■ *When* questions and simple past ■ Time phrases ■ *Someone, some, anyone, everyone,* and *no one*
Review: Units 5 and 6 pages 82–83		■ Understanding a conversation		
Unit 7 **Shopping** pages 84–95 Topic: **Comparison shopping**	■ Comparing price and quality ■ Comparing two things ■ Comparing three or more things	■ Asking and answering questions to compare furniture, appliances, and stores	■ Furniture ■ Descriptive adjectives	■ Comparatives ■ Superlatives ■ *One, the other, some, the others*
Unit 8 **Work** pages 96–107 Topic: **Work history and job skills**	■ Identifying job duties ■ Describing work history	■ Asking and answering questions about completed actions ■ Connecting ideas	■ Hospital terms ■ Job duties	■ *What* and *Where* questions and simple past ■ Conjunctions *and, or, but* ■ Past and present ability with *could, couldn't, can,* and *can't*
Review: Units 7 and 8 pages 108–109		■ Understanding a narrative		
Unit 9 **Daily living** pages 110–121 Topic: **Solving common problems**	■ Asking for recommendations ■ Requesting help politely ■ Agreeing to a request ■ Refusing a request politely	■ Asking for and making recommendations ■ Explaining choices ■ Making polite requests ■ Agreeing to and refusing requests politely	■ Home problems ■ Descriptive adjectives	■ Requests with *Can, Could, Will, Would* ■ *Which* questions and simple present ■ *Let's* and *let's not*
Unit 10 **Free time** pages 122–133 Topic: **Special occasions**	■ Making offers politely ■ Responding to offers politely	■ Making offers politely ■ Responding to offers politely ■ Asking and answering questions involving direct and indirect objects	■ Celebrations ■ Party food ■ Gifts	■ *Would you like . . . ?* ■ Direct and indirect objects ■ *There is / there are* and *there was / there were*
Review: Units 9 and 10 pages 134–135		■ Understanding a conversation		

READING	WRITING	LIFE SKILLS	PRONUNCIATION
■ Reading a magazine interview ■ Skimming interview questions to determine the focus	■ Writing a narrative paragraph about important life events ■ Using a comma after a time phrase at the beginning of a sentence	■ Reading an application for a marriage license ■ Describing important life events in sequence	■ Pronouncing key vocabulary
			■ Pronouncing intonation in questions
■ Reading a short newspaper article ■ Guessing the meaning of new words from other words nearby	■ Writing a descriptive paragraph about a gift ■ Using *because* to answer *Why* and to give a reason	■ Reading a sales receipt	■ Pronouncing key vocabulary
■ Reading a letter of recommendation ■ Scanning text for names and dates	■ Writing a summary paragraph about employment history ■ Capitalizing the names of businesses	■ Reading a time sheet	■ Pronouncing key vocabulary
			■ Pronouncing the -*ed* ending in the simple past
■ Reading a notice on a notice board ■ Determining if new words are positive or negative in meaning	■ Writing a letter of complaint ■ Identifying the parts of a letter	■ Reading a customer invoice for service and repairs	■ Pronouncing key vocabulary
■ Reading a first-person narrative paragraph about a party ■ Looking for examples of the main idea while reading	■ Writing a thank-you note for a gift ■ Indenting paragraphs in an informal note	■ Reading a formal invitation to a party	■ Pronouncing key vocabulary
			■ Pronouncing the -*s* ending in the simple present

To the teacher

What is *Ventures*?

Ventures is a six-level, four-skills, standards-based, integrated-skills series that empowers students to achieve their academic and career goals.

- This most complete program with a wealth of resources provides instructors with the tools for any teaching situation.
- The new Online Workbook keeps students learning outside the classroom.
- Easy-to-teach materials make for a more productive classroom.

What components does *Ventures* have?

Student's Book with Audio CD

Each of the core **Student's Books** contains ten topic-focused units, interspersed with five review units. The main units feature six skill-focused lessons.

- **Lessons** in the Student's Book are self-contained, allowing for completion within a one-hour class period.
- **Review lessons** recycle and reinforce the listening, vocabulary, and grammar skills developed in the two prior units and include a pronunciation activity.
- **Self-assessments** in the back of the book give students an opportunity to reflect on their learning. They support learner persistence and help determine whether students are ready for the unit test.
- **Reference charts**, also in the back of the book, provide grammar paradigms; rules for spelling, punctuation, and grammar; and lists of ordinal numbers, cardinal numbers, countries, and nationalities.
- References to the **Self-study audio CD** that accompanies the Student's Book are indicated in the Student's Book by an icon and track number: Look for the audio icon and track number to find activities with self-study audio. "STUDENT" refers to the self-study audio, and "CLASS" refers to the class audio. A full class audio is available separately.

STUDENT TK 10
CLASS CD1 TK 14

- A **Student Arcade**, available online at www.cambridge.org/venturesarcade, allows students to practice their skills with interactive activities and download self-study audio.

Teacher's Edition with Assessment Audio CD / CD-ROM

The interleaved **Teacher's Edition** includes easy-to-follow lesson plans for every unit.

- Tips and suggestions address common areas of difficulty for students and provide suggestions for expansion activities and improving learner persistence.
- A **More Ventures** chart at the end of each lesson indicates where to find additional practice material in other *Ventures* components such as the Workbook, Online Teacher's Resource Room (see below), and Student Arcade.
- Unit, midterm, and final tests, which include listening, vocabulary, grammar, reading, and writing sections, are found in the back of the Teacher's Edition.
- The **Assessment Audio CD / CD-ROM** that accompanies the Teacher's Edition contains the audio for each unit, midterm, and final test. It also features all the tests in customizable format so teachers can customize them to suit their needs.

Online Teacher's Resource Room (www.cambridge.org/myresourceroom)

Ventures 2nd Edition offers a free Online Teacher's Resource Room where teachers can download hundreds of additional worksheets and classroom materials including:

- A *placement test* that helps place students into appropriate levels of *Ventures*.
- A *Career and Educational Pathways* solution that helps students identify their educational and career goals.
- *Collaborative activities* for each lesson in Levels 1–4 that develop cooperative learning and community building within the classroom.
- *Writing worksheets* that help Literacy-level students recognize and write shapes, letters, and numbers, while alphabet and number cards promote partner and group work.
- *Picture dictionary cards and worksheets* that reinforce vocabulary learned in Levels Basic, 1, and 2.
- *Extended readings and worksheets* that provide added reading skills development for Levels 3 and 4.
- **Add Ventures** worksheets that were designed for use in multilevel classrooms and in leveled classes where the proficiency level of students differs.

Log on to www.cambridge.org/myresourceroom to explore these and hundreds of other free resources.

Workbook with Audio CD

The **Workbook** provides two pages of activities for each lesson in the Student's Book and includes an audio CD.

- If used in class, the Workbook can extend classroom instructional time by 30 minutes per lesson.
- The exercises are designed so learners can complete them in class or independently. Students can check their answers with the answer key in the back of the Workbook. Workbook exercises can be assigned in class, for homework, or as student support when a class is missed.
- Grammar charts at the back of the Workbook allow students to use the Workbook for self-study.

Online Workbooks

The self-grading **Online Workbooks** offer programs the flexibility of introducing blended learning.

- They provide the same high-quality practice opportunities as the print Workbooks and give students instant feedback.
- They allow teachers and programs to track student progress and time on task.

Unit organization

Each unit has six skill-focused lessons:

LESSON A Listening focuses students on the unit topic. The initial exercise, **Before you listen**, creates student interest with visuals that help the teacher assess what learners already know and serve as a prompt for the unit's key vocabulary. Next is **Listen**, which is based on conversations. Students relate vocabulary to meaning and relate the spoken and written forms of new theme-related vocabulary. **After you listen** concludes the lesson by practicing language related to the theme in a communicative activity, either orally with a partner or individually in a writing activity.

LESSONS B AND C focus on grammar. The lessons move from a **Grammar focus** that presents the grammar point in chart form; to **Practice** exercises that check comprehension of the grammar point and provide guided practice; and, finally, to **Communicate** exercises that guide learners as they generate original answers and conversations. These lessons often include a *Culture note*, which provides information directly related to the conversation practice (such as the use of titles with last names), or a *Useful language* note, which introduces useful expressions and functional language.

LESSON D Reading develops reading skills and expands vocabulary. The lesson opens with a **Before you read** exercise, designed to activate prior knowledge and encourage learners to make predictions. A *Reading tip*, which focuses on a specific reading skill, accompanies the **Read** exercise. The reading section of the lesson concludes with **After you read** exercises that check comprehension. In Levels Basic, 1, and 2, the vocabulary expansion portion of the lesson is a **Picture dictionary**. It includes a *word bank*, pictures to identify, and a conversation for practicing the new words. The words expand vocabulary related to the unit topic. In Books 3 and 4, the vocabulary expansion portion of the lesson uses new vocabulary from the reading to build skills such as recognizing word families, selecting definitions based on the context of the reading, and using clues in the reading to guess meaning.

LESSON E Writing provides practice with process writing within the context of the unit. **Before you write** exercises provide warm-up activities to activate the language needed for the writing assignment, followed by one or more exercises that provide a model for students to follow when they write. A *Writing tip* presents information about punctuation or paragraph organization directly related to the writing assignment. The **Write** exercise sets goals for the student writing. In the **After you write** exercise, students share with a partner.

LESSON F Another view has three sections. *Life-skills reading* develops the scanning and skimming skills used with documents such as forms, charts, schedules, announcements, and ads. Multiple-choice questions (modeled on CASAS[1] and BEST[2]) develop test-taking skills. *Grammar connections*, in Levels 1–4, contrasts grammar points and includes guided practice and communicative activities. Finally, *Wrap up* refers students to the self-assessment page in the back of the book, where they can check their knowledge and evaluate their progress.

---

[1] The Comprehensive Adult Student Assessment System. For more information, see www.casas.org.
[2] The Basic English Skills Test. For more information, see www.cal.org/BEST.

Unit tour

The Most Complete Course for Student Success

Ventures empowers students to achieve their academic and career goals.

- ■ The most complete program with a wealth of resources provides instructors with the tools for any teaching situation.
- ■ The new Online Workbook keeps students learning outside the classroom.
- ■ Easy-to-teach materials make for a more productive classroom.

The Big Picture

- • Introduces the unit topic and provides rich opportunities for classroom discussion.
- • Activates students' prior knowledge and previews the unit vocabulary.

Unit Goals

- • Explicit unit goals ensure student involvement in the learning process.

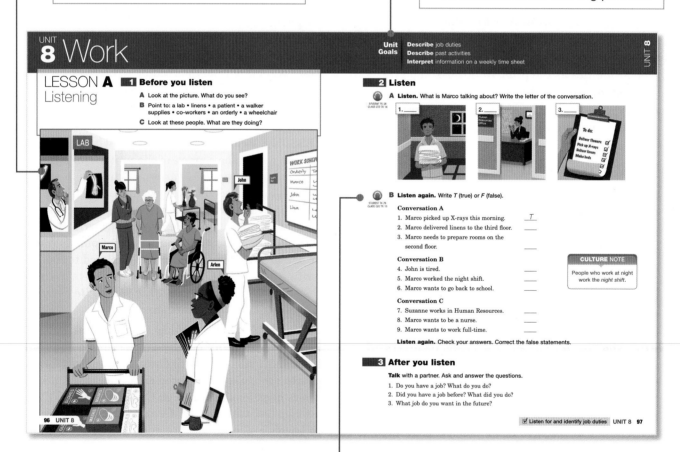

Two Different Audio Programs

- • Class audio features over 100 minutes of listening practice to improve listening comprehension.
- • Self-study audio encourages learner persistence and autonomy.
- • Easy navigation between the two with clear track listings.

Grammar Chart

- Clear grammar charts with additional grammar reference in the back of the book allow for greater teacher flexibility.

Natural Progression

- Students gain fluency and confidence by moving from guided practice to communicative activities.

Real-life Practice

- Meaningful application of the grammar allows for better student engagement.

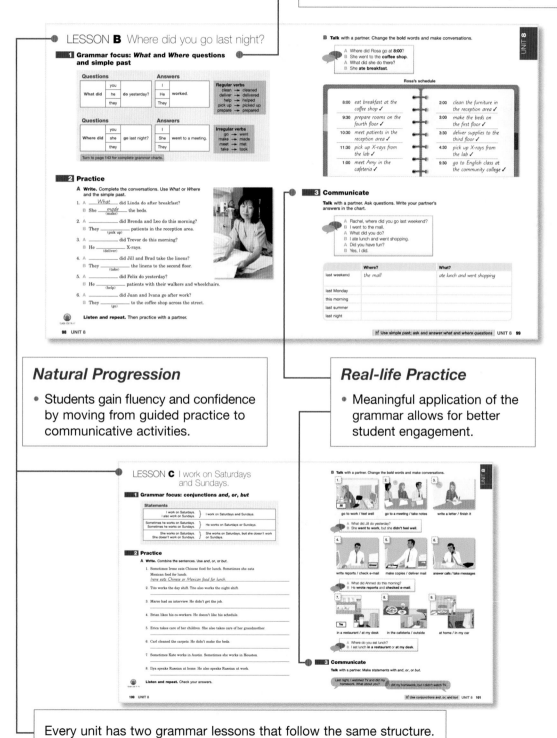

Every unit has two grammar lessons that follow the same structure.

Reading

- *Ventures* features a three-step reading approach that highlights reading strategies and skills needed for success: **Before you read, Read, After you read.**

Integrated-skills Approach

- Reading is combined with writing and listening for an integrated approach that ensures better comprehension.

Picture Dictionary

- This visual page expands unit vocabulary and works on pronunciation for richer understanding of the topic.

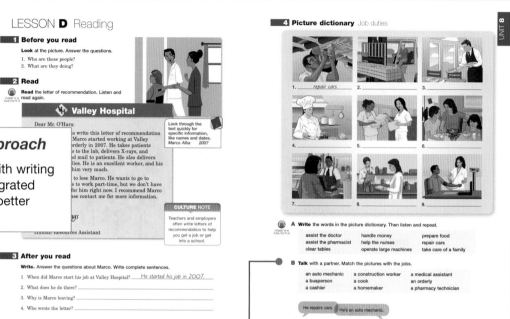

Process Writing

- *Ventures* includes a robust process-writing approach: prewriting, writing, and peer review.

Talk with a Partner

- Spoken practice helps students internalize the vocabulary and relate it to their lives.

Writing for Success

- *Ventures* writing lessons are academic and purposeful, which moves students toward work and educational goals.

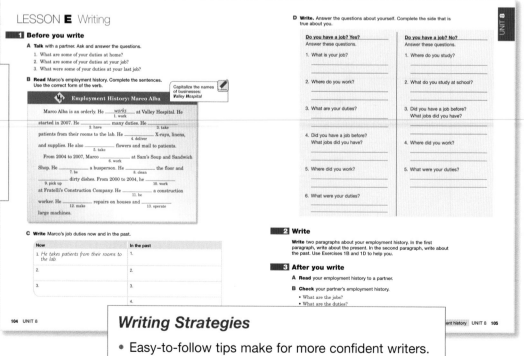

Writing Strategies

- Easy-to-follow tips make for more confident writers.

Document Literacy

- Explicit practice with authentic-type documents builds real-life skills.

Grammar Connections

- Contrasting two grammar forms in a communicative way helps with grammar accuracy.

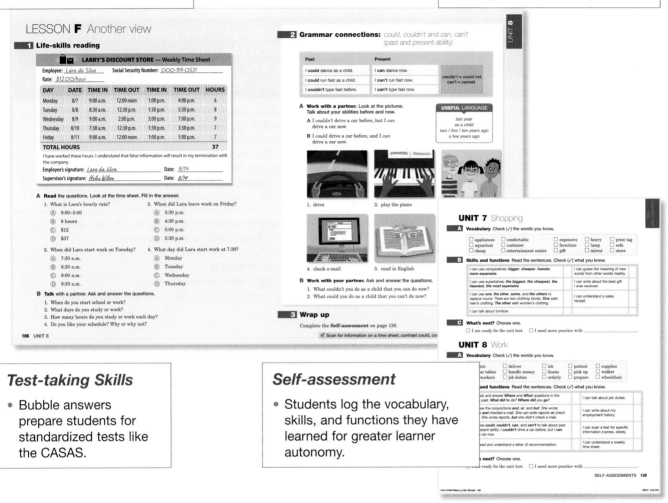

Test-taking Skills

- Bubble answers prepare students for standardized tests like the CASAS.

Self-assessment

- Students log the vocabulary, skills, and functions they have learned for greater learner autonomy.

Review

- An integrated-skills approach reinforces the language of the previous two units.

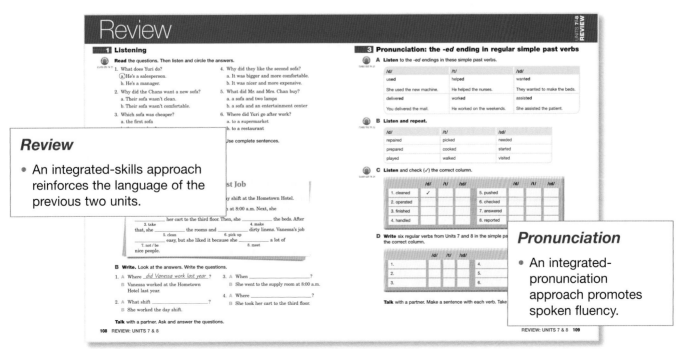

Pronunciation

- An integrated-pronunciation approach promotes spoken fluency.

Correlations

UNIT	CASAS Competencies	NRS EDUCATIONAL Functioning Level Descriptors *Oral BEST: 29–41 (SPL 3)* *BEST Plus: 418–438 (SPL 3)* *BEST Literacy: 36–46 (SPL 3)*
Unit 1 **Personal information** Pages 6–17	0.1.2, 0.1.4, 0.1.5, 0.1.6, 0.2.1, 0.2.3, 0.2.4, 1.1.6, 1.1.9, 1.2.1, 1.2.5, 1.3.1, 1.3.3, 1.3.4, 1.3.9, 1.6.4, 2.4.2, 2.6.1, 4.8.1, 4.8.2, 4.8.3, 6.0.2, 7.2.1, 7.4.7, 7.5.1, 8.1.2, 8.1.4	▪ Common words, simple phrases, and sentences ▪ Answering simple questions about everyday activities ▪ Reading sight words and common vocabulary ▪ Reading familiar phrases and simple sentences ▪ Writing simple sentences ▪ Working with others in social situations ▪ Providing basic personal information on forms
Unit 2 **At school** Pages 18–29	0.1.2, 0.1.4, 0.1.5, 0.2.1, 0.2.4, 1.2.1, 1.9.6, 2.3.2, 2.5.5, 4.1.4, 4.1.6, 4.1.7, 4.1.8, 4.1.9, 4.4.2, 4.4.5, 4.8.1, 4.8.2, 7.1.1, 7.1.4, 7.2.2, 7.2.6, 7.3.1, 7.3.2, 7.3.4, 7.4.2, 7.4.7, 7.4.8, 7.5.1, 7.5.7, 8.3.2	▪ Answering simple questions about everyday activities ▪ Using simple phrases and short sentences ▪ Reading sight words and common vocabulary ▪ Writing simple sentences ▪ Practicing writing with correct grammar ▪ Recognizing forms at home, work, and in the community
Unit 3 **Friends and family** Pages 32–43	0.1.2, 0.1.4, 0.1.5, 0.2.1, 0.2.4, 1.2.1, 1.2.2, 1.2.4, 1.2.5, 1.5.2, 2.1.4, 2.6.1, 4.8.1, 4.8.2, 4.8.4, 6.0.1, 6.0.2, 6.0.3, 6.0.4, 6.1.1, 6.1.3, 6.2.3, 6.5.1, 6.6.6, 7.1.4, 7.2.1, 7.2.7, 7.3.2, 7.4.2, 7.4.3, 7.4.7, 7.5.1, 8.1.2, 8.2.1, 8.2.2, 8.2.3, 8.2.4	▪ Expressing immediate needs ▪ Expanding understanding of grammar ▪ Reading sight and common words ▪ Reading familiar phrases ▪ Practicing writing with correct grammar ▪ Working with others in social situations ▪ Recognizing forms at home, work, and in the community
Unit 4 **Health** Pages 44–55	0.1.2, 0.1.4, 0.1.5, 0.2.1, 1.2.5, 3.1.1, 3.2.1, 3.3.1, 3.3.2, 3.4.1, 3.4.2, 3.4.3, 3.5.9, 4.3.3, 4.8.1, 7.1.4, 7.2.1, 7.3.2, 7.4.2, 7.4.7	▪ Answering simple questions about everyday activities ▪ Expressing immediate needs ▪ Expanding understanding of grammar ▪ Reading sight and common words ▪ Reading familiar phrases ▪ Writing simple sentences ▪ Recognizing common forms of print
Unit 5 **Around town** Pages 58–69	0.1.2, 0.1.4, 0.1.5, 0.1.6, 0.2.1, 0.2.4, 2.2.1, 2.2.3, 2.2.4, 2.3.1, 4.8.1, 6.0.1, 6.0.2, 6.0.3, 6.0.4, 6.1.2, 6.6.6, 7.1.1, 7.4.2, 7.4.7	▪ Common words, simple phrases, and sentences ▪ Expanding understanding of grammar ▪ Reading sight words and common vocabulary ▪ Reading familiar phrases and simple sentences ▪ Practicing writing with correct grammar ▪ Recognizing forms at home, work, and in the community

All units of *Ventures 2nd Edition* meet most of the EFF content standards and provide overall BEST test preparation. The chart above lists areas of particular focus.

For more details and correlations to other state standards, go to: www.cambridge.org/myresourceroom

EFF	Florida Adult ESOL Beginning High	LAUSD ESL High Beginning Competencies
■ Conveying ideas in writing ■ Interacting with others in positive ways ■ Monitoring comprehension ■ Reading with understanding ■ Speaking so others can understand ■ Understanding and working with pictures ■ Cooperating with others	3.01.01, 3.01.03, 3.03.16, 3.04.01, 3.04.06, 3.04.08, 3.04.09	I. 1, 3, 4, 5, 6 II. 7a, 11e III. 14 IV. 27 VIII. 62
■ Conveying ideas in writing ■ Guiding others ■ Listening actively ■ Paying attention to the conventions of written English ■ Seeking input from others ■ Solving problems and making decisions ■ Cooperating with others ■ Speaking so others can understand	3.03.01, 3.03.05, 3.03.13, 3.03.14	I. 5 II. 7a III. 12, 14, 15 VIII. 59
■ Attending to oral information ■ Organizing and presenting written information ■ Paying attention to the conventions of spoken English ■ Selecting appropriate reading strategies ■ Solving problems using appropriate quantitative procedures ■ Speaking so others can understand ■ Cooperating with others	3.01.03, 3.01.08, 3.02.02, 3.02.08, 3.03.16, 3.04.01, 3.04.06, 3.05.04	II. 71 III. 17a IV. 32 VIII. 59, 62
■ Conveying ideas in writing ■ Offering clear input ■ Seeking input from others ■ Speaking so others can understand ■ Taking stock of where one is ■ Understanding and working with numbers ■ Cooperating with others	3.05.01, 3.05.04, 3.07.01	II. 7b III. 17a VI. 45, 47, 49 VII. 57
■ Conveying ideas in writing ■ Listening actively ■ Offering clear input ■ Organizing and presenting written information ■ Selecting appropriate reading strategies ■ Understanding and working with numbers and pictures ■ Cooperating with others ■ Speaking so others can understand	3.03.16, 3.04.01, 3.06.01	I. 4 II. 7b, 8c III. 23b VIII. 62

UNIT	CASAS Competencies	NRS EDUCATIONAL Functioning Level Descriptors *Oral BEST: 29–41 (SPL 3)* *BEST Plus: 418–438 (SPL 3)* *BEST Literacy: 36–46 (SPL 3)*
Unit 6 **Time** Pages 70–81	0.1.2, 0.1.4, 0.1.5, 0.2.1, 0.2.3, 0.2.4, 2.3.1, 2.3.2, 2.7.2, 4.8.1, 5.3.1, 5.3.6, 6.0.1, 7.1.1, 7.2.1, 7.2.4, 7.2.7, 7.4.2, 7.4.3, 7.4.7, 7.4.8, 7.5.1	▪ Using simple phrases and short sentences ▪ Expanding understanding of grammar ▪ Reading sight and common words ▪ Writing simple sentences ▪ Practicing writing with correct grammar ▪ Providing basic personal information on forms ▪ Recognizing forms at home, work, and in the community
Unit 7 **Shopping** Pages 84–95	0.1.2, 0.1.4, 0.1.5, 0.2.1, 1.1.6, 1.2.1, 1.2.2, 1.2.6, 1.2.7, 1.4.1, 1.6.3, 4.8.1, 6.0.1, 6.0.2, 7.1.1, 7.2.3, 7.4.2, 7.4.7, 7.5.1, 8.1.4	▪ Expressing immediate needs ▪ Expanding understanding of grammar ▪ Reading familiar phrases ▪ Writing simple sentences ▪ Practicing writing with correct grammar ▪ Working with others in social situations ▪ Recognizing forms at home, work, and in the community
Unit 8 **Work** Pages 96–107	0.1.2, 0.1.4, 0.1.5, 0.2.1, 1.1.6, 2.3.1, 2.3.2, 4.1.2, 4.1.6, 4.1.8, 4.2.1, 4.4.3, 4.5.1, 4.8.1, 4.8.2, 6.0.1, 7.1.1, 7.1.4, 7.2.1, 7.2.3, 7.4.7, 7.5.1	▪ Answering simple questions about everyday activities ▪ Reading sight words and common vocabulary ▪ Reading familiar phrases and simple sentences ▪ Writing simple sentences ▪ Providing personal information on forms ▪ Practicing entry-level job-related writing ▪ Practicing entry-level job-related speaking
Unit 9 **Daily living** Pages 110–121	0.1.2, 0.1.4, 0.1.5, 0.2.1, 0.2.3, 1.1.6, 1.4.1, 1.4.5, 1.4.7, 1.5.2 , 1.6.3, 1.7.4, 1.7.5, 4.1.8, 4.8.1, 4.8.6, 6.0.1, 7.1.1, 7.1.2, 7.2.1, 7.2.2, 7.3.2, 7.3.4, 7.4.2, 7.4.7, 7.5.1, 7.5.6, 8.1.4, 8.2.6, 8.3.1, 8.3.2	▪ Expressing immediate needs ▪ Using simple phrases and short sentences ▪ Expanding understanding of grammar ▪ Reading familiar phrases and simple sentences ▪ Writing simple sentences ▪ Practicing writing with correct grammar ▪ Working with others in social situations
Unit 10 **Free time** Pages 122–133	0.1.2, 0.1.4, 0.1.5, 0.2.1, 0.2.3, 0.2.4, 2.3.1, 2.3.2, 2.6.1, 2.7.1, 2.7.2, 4.8.1, 4.8.3, 7.1.1, 7.2.1, 7.4.7, 7.5.1, 7.5.6	▪ Common words, simple phrases, and sentences ▪ Expanding understanding of grammar ▪ Writing simple sentences ▪ Practicing writing with correct grammar ▪ Practicing correct punctuation ▪ Working with others in social situations ▪ Recognizing forms at home, work, and in the community

All units of *Ventures 2nd Edition* meet most of the EFF content standards and provide overall BEST test preparation. The chart above lists areas of particular focus.

For more details and correlations to other state standards, go to: www.cambridge.org/myresourceroom

EFF	Florida Adult ESOL Beginning High	LAUSD ESL High Beginning Competencies
▪ Conveying ideas in writing ▪ Cooperating with others ▪ Paying attention to the conventions of spoken English ▪ Reading with understanding ▪ Reflecting and evaluating ▪ Understanding and working with numbers and pictures ▪ Speaking so others can understand	3.03.01, 3.03.09, 3.04.01	I. 4, 5 II. 7a III. 5 VIII. 62
▪ Attending to oral information ▪ Attending to visual sources of information ▪ Identifying strengths and weaknesses as a learner ▪ Making inferences, predictions, or judgments ▪ Seeking feedback and revising accordingly ▪ Taking responsibility for learning ▪ Cooperating with others ▪ Speaking so others can understand	3.03.01, 3.04.01, 3.04.06, 3.06.03	III. 23b IV. 27, 30, 32 VIII. 62
▪ Listening actively ▪ Monitoring comprehension and adjusting reading strategies ▪ Organizing and presenting written information ▪ Setting and prioritizing goals ▪ Speaking so others can understand ▪ Testing out new learning in real-life applications ▪ Cooperating with others	3.01.03, 3.03.01, 3.03.13, 3.03.14, 3.03.16	I. 5 II. 7a, 7b, 8a, 8b, 22 III. 25 VIII. 62
▪ Anticipating and identifying problems ▪ Conveying ideas in writing ▪ Engaging parties in trying to reach agreement ▪ Reading with understanding ▪ Setting and prioritizing goals ▪ Speaking so others can understand ▪ Cooperating with others	3.01.02, 3.04.05, 3.04.06	II. 7a, 7b, 9b, 9c, 10a III. 25 V. 27, 32, 39
▪ Cooperating with others ▪ Identifying strengths and weaknesses as a learner ▪ Paying attention to the conventions of spoken English ▪ Reflecting and evaluating ▪ Testing out new learning in real-life applications ▪ Understanding and working with pictures and numbers ▪ Speaking so others can understand	3.01.02, 3.03.16	II. 10a

Meet the *Ventures* author team

Gretchen Bitterlin has been an ESL teacher and an ESL department chair. She is currently the ESL coordinator for the Continuing Education Program at San Diego Community College District. Under Gretchen's leadership, the ESL program has developed several products – for example, an ESL oral interview placement test and writing rubrics for assessing writing for level exit – now used by other agencies. She is a co-author of *English for Adult Competency*, has been an item writer for CASAS tests, and chaired the task force that developed the TESOL *Adult Education Program Standards*. She is a recipient of her district's award, Outstanding Contract Faculty. Gretchen holds an MA in TESOL from the University of Arizona.

Dennis Johnson had his first language-teaching experience as a Peace Corps volunteer in South Korea. Following that teaching experience, he became an in-country ESL trainer. After returning to the United States, he became an ESL trainer and began teaching credit and non-credit ESL at City College of San Francisco. As ESL site coordinator, he has provided guidance to faculty in selecting textbooks. He is the author of *Get Up and Go* and co-author of *The Immigrant Experience*. Dennis is the demonstration teacher on the *Ventures Professional Development DVD*. Dennis holds an MA in music from Stanford University.

Donna Price began her ESL career teaching EFL in Madagascar. She is currently associate professor of ESL and vocational ESL / technology resource instructor for the Continuing Education Program, San Diego Community College District. She has served as an author and a trainer for CALPRO, the California Adult Literacy Professional Development Project, co-authoring training modules on contextualizing and integrating workforce skills into the ESL classroom. She is a recipient of the TESOL Newbury House Award for Excellence in Teaching, and she is author of *Skills for Success*. Donna holds an MA in linguistics from San Diego State University.

Sylvia Ramirez started as an instructional aide in ESL. Since then she has been a part-time teacher, a full-time teacher, and a program coordinator. As program coordinator at Mira Costa College, she provided leadership in establishing Managed Enrollment, Student Learning Outcomes, and Transitioning Adults to Academic and Career Preparation. Her more than forty years in adult ESL includes multilevel ESL, vocational ESL, family literacy, and distance learning. She has also provided technical assistance to local ESL programs for the California State Department of Education. In 2011 she received the Hayward Award in education. Her MA is in education / counseling from Point Loma University, and she has certificates in TESOL and in online teaching.

K. Lynn Savage first taught English in Japan. She began teaching ESL at City College of San Francisco in 1974, where she has taught all levels of non-credit ESL and has served as Vocational ESL Resource Teacher. She has trained teachers for adult education programs around the country as well as abroad. She chaired the committee that developed *ESL Model Standards for Adult Education Programs* (California, 1992) and is the author, co-author, and editor of many ESL materials including *Crossroads Café*, *Teacher Training through Video*, *Parenting for Academic Success*, *Building Life Skills*, *Picture Stories*, *May I Help You?*, and *English That Works*. Lynn holds an MA in TESOL from Teachers College, Columbia University.

To the student

Welcome to **Ventures**! The dictionary says that "venture" means a risky or daring journey. Its meaning is similar to the word "adventure." Learning English is certainly a journey and an adventure. We hope that this book helps you in your journey of learning English to fulfill your goals. We believe that this book will prepare you for academic and career courses and give you the English skills you need to get a job or promotion, go to college, or communicate better in your community. The CDs, the workbooks, and the free Internet practice on the Arcade will help you improve your English outside class. Setting your personal goals will also help. Take a few minutes and write down your goals below.

Good luck in your studies!

The Author Team
Gretchen Bitterlin
Dennis Johnson
Donna Price
Sylvia Ramirez
K. Lynn Savage

My goals for studying English

1. My first goal for studying English:	Date: _____
2. My second goal for studying English:	Date: _____
3. My third goal for studying English:	Date: _____

Welcome

1 Meet your classmates

A Look at the picture. What do you see?

B What are the people doing?

2 Skills

A Listen. Amanda is in class. A classmate is interviewing her about her skills. Check (✓) the things Amanda can do.

STUDENT TK 2
CLASS CD1 TK 2

✓ use a computer   _____ read to children   _____ write in English

_____ speak English   _____ speak Spanish   _____ speak Russian

Listen again. Check your answers.

B Read the list. Check (✓) the things you can do. Add two more skills.

Things I can do in English	
✓ introduce myself	☐ help my child with homework
☐ say my address and telephone number	☐ read to my child
☐ register for a class	☐ read a class schedule
☐ make an appointment with a doctor	☐ read a television schedule
☐ give directions	☐ talk about my weekend
☐ write a shopping list	_____
☐ ask about prices	_____

Talk with a partner. Share your information.

C Talk with your classmates. Find classmates with these skills. Complete the chart.

Armin, can you swim?

Yes, I can.

Ask: Can you ...	Classmate's name
swim?	*Armin*
iron a shirt?	
cook?	
drive a truck?	
paint a house?	
speak three languages?	

USEFUL LANGUAGE

How do you spell that?

Talk with your class. Ask and answer questions.

Who can swim?

Armin can.

Ali can, too.

3 Verb tense review (present and past of be)

A Listen to each sentence. Check (✓) the correct column.

STUDENT TK 3
CLASS CD1 TK 3

	am	is	are	was	were
1.	✓				
2.					
3.					
4.					
5.					
6.					
7.					

Listen again. Check your answers.

B Read about Maria. Complete the story. Use *am, is, are, was, were,* and *weren't.*

My name _____is_____ Maria. I _____
         1.   2.
from Mexico. My husband's name _____
                                        3.
Sergio. He _____ from Mexico, too. There
            4.
_____ three children in our family –
   5.
one son and two daughters. Our son, Javier,

_____ seven years old. He _____
   6.   7.
born in Mexico. Our daughters, Melisa and Maritza,

_____ twins. They _____ four years
   8.   9.
old. They _____ born in the United States. Sergio and I _____ born in the
      10.   11.
United States. We _____ born in Mexico.
      12.

Listen and check your answers.

STUDENT TK 4
CLASS CD1 TK 4

C Talk with a partner. Ask and answer the questions. Take turns.

1. Where are you from?
2. Were you born there?
3. What was your occupation there?
4. Are you married?
5. How many people are in your family?
6. Is your family here with you?

Share your information with the class.

4 Verb tense review (present and past of regular and irregular verbs)

STUDENT TK 5
CLASS CD1 TK 5

A **Listen** to each sentence. For each, circle the verb you hear.

Regular and irregular verbs

Present	Past	Present	Past
1. (takes)	took	6. takes	took
2. work	worked	7. doesn't buy	didn't buy
3. visits	visited	8. wants	wanted
4. celebrate	celebrated	9. sleeps	slept
5. goes	went	10. don't walk	didn't walk

Listen again. Check your answers.

B **Read** the conversation. Fill in the missing words. Use the correct verb form.

A When did you ___come___ to this country?
   1. come

B I ___came___ here two years ago.
   2. come

A You speak very well. Did you ___study___ English here last year?
   3. study

B Yes, I ___did___ .
   4. do

A Did you ___speak___ English in your native country?
   5. speak

B No, I ___didn't speak___ .
   6. do

A What do you usually ___do___ on the weekend?
   7. do

B I usually ___stay___ home, but sometimes I ___go___ shopping.
   8. stay   9. go

STUDENT TK 6
CLASS CD1 TK 6

Listen and check your answers.

C **Talk** with your classmates. Ask and answer the questions. Take turns.

1. What do you usually do on the weekend?
2. What did you do last weekend?
3. When did you come to this country?

Share your information with the class.

Personal information

LESSON A
Listening

1 Before you listen

A Look at the picture. What do you see?

B Point to: long brown hair • straight hair • a jogging suit
curly blond hair • short hair • a red shirt • a striped skirt

C Describe the people. What are they doing?

Unit Goals

Describe people

Identify clothing items

Interpret information on an order form

---

2 Listen

A **Listen.** Who is Shoko talking about? Write the letter of the conversation.

STUDENT TK 7
CLASS CD1 TK 7

1. _____

2. _a_

3. _____

B **Listen again.** Write *T* (true) or *F* (false).

STUDENT TK 7
CLASS CD1 TK 7

Conversation A

1. Victoria is Shoko's daughter.   _T_

2. Victoria plays soccer every day.   _____

3. Victoria looks like her mother.   _____

Conversation B

4. Eddie is Shoko's brother.   _____

5. Eddie has a lot of friends.   _____

6. Eddie is a very quiet boy.   _____

Conversation C

7. Mark is Shoko's husband.   _____

8. Mark is a short man.   _____

9. Mark studies Spanish.   _____

Listen again. Check your answers.

3 After you listen

Talk with a partner. Describe someone in your family.

> My mother has long blond hair.

> My mother has curly brown hair.

☑ Listen for and identify people and information about them   **UNIT 1**   **7**

LESSON **B** She's wearing a short plaid skirt.

1 Grammar focus: adjective order

Question

What's she wearing?

Answers

She's wearing **a short plaid** skirt.
a long black and white coat.

Adjective order

Size	Color		Pattern
small	black	purple	
large	blue	red	
short	brown	yellow	
long	green	white	

checked　　plaid　　striped

Turn to page 146 for an additional adjective order chart.

2 Practice

A Write. Complete the conversations. Write the words in the correct order.

1. **A** What's Amy wearing?

    B She's wearing a _____*long*_____ _____*black*_____ dress.
    (black / long)

2. **A** What's she wearing?

    B She's wearing _____ _____ pants.
    (black and white / checked)

3. **A** What does he take to school?

    B He takes a _____ _____ backpack.
    (large / red)

4. **A** What do you usually wear to work?

    B I wear a _____ _____ uniform.
    (blue and white / striped)

5. **A** What's he wearing today?

    B He's wearing a _____ _____ sweater.
    (plaid / red and yellow)

6. **A** What are they wearing?

    B They're wearing _____ _____ skirts.
    (green / short)

Listen and repeat. Then practice with a partner.

B **Write** the letter. What are the people wearing?

a. blue plaid pants
b. a long purple coat
c. red shoes
d. a blue checked skirt
e. a short striped dress
f. long black boots
g. a long yellow shirt
h. red and white striped socks
i. a brown sweater
j. a green plaid suit

Talk with a partner. Change the **bold** words and make conversations.

A What's **Lisa** wearing?
B **She's** wearing a **long yellow shirt**.

> **USEFUL** LANGUAGE
>
> Some clothing items are always plural: *jeans, pants,* and *shorts.*

3 Communicate

Talk with a partner about your classmates.

What's Maya wearing?

She's wearing jeans and a long green sweater.

☑ Use correct order with two or more adjectives   **UNIT 1**   **9**

LESSON C What are you doing right now?

1 Grammar focus: present continuous and simple present

Present continuous questions			Answers			Time words
What **are** you What**'s** he What **are** they	**doing**	right now? today?	I'm He's They're	**watching** TV.		now right now today

Simple present questions			Answers					Time words
What	**do** you **do** **does** she **do** **do** they **do**	every Tuesday? every day?	I She They	always usually	**go** **goes** **go**	to the park.		always usually every day

Turn to page 141 for a complete grammar chart.

2 Practice

A Write. Complete the conversations. Use the correct form of the verb.

1. **A** What ___does___ Ed ___do___ every night?
       (do)

   B He ___relaxes___ .
       (relax)

   A What ___is___ Ed ___doing___ right now?
       (do)

   B He___'s watching___ TV.
       (watch)

2. **A** What ___is___ Mary ___doing___ right now?
       (do)

   B She ___is teaching___
       (teach)

   A What ___does___ Mary ___do___ every Tuesday?
       (do)

   B She ___teaches___ .
       (teach)

3. **A** What ___is___ Isaac ___doing___ right now?
       (do)

   B He___'s studying___ .
       (study)

   A What ___does___ Isaac ___do___ every day?
       (do)

   B He ___goes___ to class.
       (go)

Listen and repeat. Then practice with a partner.

CLASS CD1 TK 9

10 UNIT 1

B **Talk** with a partner. Change the **bold** words and make conversations.

A Look! **Betty is leaving early!**
B Of course. **She leaves early** every night.

1. Betty / leave early
2. Henry / call his wife
3. Jin-ho / study alone

4. Olga and Yuri / speak English
5. Yan and Ling / drink coffee
6. Antonio / wear jeans and a tie

3 Communicate

A **Talk** with a partner. Ask and answer questions about your routines.

A What do you do on the weekend?
B I usually do things with my children.

A What do you do every night?
B I always study English.

B **Talk** in a group. Ask and answer questions about your classmates right now.

A What's Sara doing right now?
B She's talking to Samuel and Kwan.

☑ Contrast present continuous and simple present   **UNIT 1**   **11**

LESSON **D** Reading

1 Before you read

Look at the picture. Answer the questions.

1. Who is the girl?
2. What is she wearing?
3. What is she doing?

2 Read

STUDENT TK 8
CLASS CD1 TK 10

Read Shoko's e-mail. Listen and read again.

New Message

From: Shoko

To: Karin

Subject: Victoria

Hi Karin,

How are you doing? Guess what! Today is my daughter's birthday. The last time you saw Victoria, she was three years old. Now she's 17! She's tall and very athletic. She likes sports. She plays soccer every afternoon. Here is her photo. She's wearing her red and white striped soccer uniform. She usually wears jeans and a T-shirt. Victoria is also a very good student. She has lots of friends and goes with them to the mall every weekend. How are your daughters? Please send a photo!

Let's stay in touch.

Shoko

> Look for a key word or words in the question, and read quickly to find the answer.
> How *old* is Victoria?

3 After you read

A **Write.** Answer the questions about Victoria. Write complete sentences.

1. How old is Victoria? _She's 17._
2. When does she go to the mall? _____
3. What sport does she play? _____
4. What kind of student is Victoria? _____
5. What does she usually wear? _____

B **Write.** Complete the sentences about Victoria.

1. Victoria is very _athletic_ .
2. She likes _____ .
3. She has lots of _____ .
4. She's wearing _____ .

4 **Picture dictionary** Accessories

1. ___a hat___
2. _____
3. _____

Ben

Sally

4. _____
5. _____

6. _____
7. _____
12. _____

Angie

8. _____
9. _____
10. _____
11. _____

A **Write** the words in the picture dictionary. Then listen and repeat.

STUDENT TK 9
CLASS CD1 TK 11

a belt	earrings	a hat	a purse	a scarf	a tie
a bracelet	gloves	a necklace	a ring	sunglasses	a watch

B **Talk** with a partner. Change the **bold** words and make conversations.

A What's Ben wearing?
B He's wearing **a red and green striped tie.**

A What's Sally wearing?
B She's wearing **a green and black checked scarf**.

☑ Read an e-mail describing a person; use vocabulary for personal accessories   **UNIT 1**   **13**

LESSON E Writing

1 Before you write

A Write. Answer the questions about yourself.

1. What's your name? _____
2. What color is your hair? _____
3. What color are your eyes? _____
4. What are you wearing? _____
5. What do you do after class? _____
6. What do you do on the weekend? _____

B Read about a new classmate.

Introducing:
Ricardo Roldan

Ricardo is a new student in our English class. He has short gray hair and brown eyes. Today he is wearing dark blue pants, a plaid shirt, and black shoes. He is also wearing a watch. He is very friendly. After class, Ricardo goes to work. On the weekend, Ricardo helps his wife and fixes things around the house. He also relaxes on the weekend.

C Write. Answer the questions about Ricardo. Write complete sentences.

1. Does Ricardo have gray hair or brown hair?

   He has gray hair. _____

2. Is his hair long or short?

   _____

3. What is he wearing?

   _____

4. What does he do on the weekend?

   _____

D **Write** each sentence in a different way.

1. After class, Ricardo goes to work.
   Ricardo goes to work after class.

> Time phrases like *after class* or *on the weekend* can come at the beginning or end of a sentence. Use a comma if they are at the beginning.

2. Tanya goes shopping on the weekend.

_____

3. Victoria plays soccer every Tuesday.

_____

4. After work, Henry watches TV.

_____

5. On the weekend, Yan studies English.

_____

E **Talk** with a partner. Complete the chart. Use the questions in Exercise 1A.

Partner's name:	
Hair color:	
Eye color:	
Clothing:	
Accessories:	
After-class activities:	
Weekend activities:	

2 Write

Write a paragraph about your partner. Use Exercises 1B and 1E to help you.

3 After you write

A **Read** your paragraph to your partner.

B **Check** your partner's paragraph.

- What did your partner write about you?
- Is the information correct?
- Are the time phrases correct?

LESSON F Another view

1 Life-skills reading

ORDER FORM

ITEM NUMBER	QUANTITY	SIZE	COLOR	ITEM NAME	PRICE
105B	1	L	RED	SWEATER	$29.00
265A	1	M	PURPLE	COAT	$69.00
350G	2	XXL	WHITE	T-SHIRT	$18.00
670F	1	8	BLACK	SHOES	$59.00

METHOD OF PAYMENT

☐ Global Express   ☐ Discovery
☑ Master Charge   ☐ Personal check
☐ Vista

CREDIT CARD ACCOUNT NUMBER:
123-1234-123

EXPIRATION DATE:
12/2015

SIGNATURE:
Phong Nguyen

SUBTOTAL	$175.00
SHIPPING AND HANDLING	$15.00

Under $50 ....$5.00
$50-$100...........$10.00
Over $100 ....$15.00

EXPRESS DELIVERY
(ADD $5.00)

TOTAL	$190.00

USEFUL LANGUAGE

S	small
M	medium
L	large
XL	extra large
XXL	extra extra large

A Read the questions. Look at the order form. Fill in the answer.

1. How much is the large red sweater?
   - Ⓐ $18.00
   - ● $29.00
   - Ⓒ $59.00
   - Ⓓ $69.00

2. What color are the shoes?
   - Ⓐ black
   - Ⓑ purple
   - Ⓒ red
   - Ⓓ white

3. What is the method of payment?
   - Ⓐ Discovery
   - Ⓑ Global Express
   - Ⓒ Master Charge
   - Ⓓ Vista

4. How much is shipping and handling?
   - Ⓐ $5.00
   - Ⓑ $10.00
   - Ⓒ $15.00
   - Ⓓ $150.00

B Talk in a group. Ask and answer the questions.

1. Where do you shop for clothing?
2. What clothes do you usually buy?
3. How do you usually pay?

2 Grammar connections: *and … too, and … either, and but*

Use *and … too* to show agreement with affirmative sentences.	David likes sports, **and** Kyle likes sports, **too**. or David likes sports, **and** Kyle does, **too**.
Use *and … either* to show agreement with negative sentences.	David doesn't wear glasses, **and** Kyle doesn't wear glasses **either**. or David doesn't wear glasses, **and** Kyle doesn't **either**.
Use *but* to show a difference.	Elsa wears glasses, **but** David doesn't wear glasses. or Elsa wears glasses, **but** David doesn't.

A Work in a group. Ask questions and complete the chart.

A Do you wear glasses, David? | **A** Do you wear glasses, Kyle?

B No, I don't. | **C** No, I don't.

	_____ (name)	_____ (name)	_____ (name)
1. Do you wear glasses?			
2. Do you like sports?			
3. Do you have a job?			
4. Do you usually eat breakfast?			
5. Do you watch TV every night?			
6. Do you usually wear a scarf?			
7. Do you usually wear a hat?			
8. Do you usually wear a watch?			

B Work with another group. Talk about two people from your group.

> David doesn't wear glasses, *and* Kyle doesn't *either*. David likes sports, *and* Kyle does, *too*.

3 Wrap up

Complete the **Self-assessment** on page 136.

LESSON A
Listening

1 **Before you listen**

A Look at the picture. What do you see?

B Point to: an English teacher • a computer lab • a hall • a monitor
a lab instructor • an ESL classroom • a keyboard • a mouse

C Look at the people. What are they doing?

Mrs. Lee

Registration Office

Computer Lab

Mr. Stephens

ESL Class

Group 1:
Computers

Group 2:
Page 18

Joseph

Eva

Unit Goals

Identify future plans
Set short-term goals
Interpret information in a course catalog

UNIT 2

2 Listen

STUDENT TK 10
CLASS CD1 TK 12

A Listen. Who is Joseph talking to? Write the letter of the conversation.

1. _____

2. _____

3. _____

STUDENT TK 10
CLASS CD1 TK 12

B Listen again. Write *T* (true) or *F* (false).

Conversation A

1. Eva and Joseph are in the computer lab.   *F*

2. Mrs. Lee helped Eva.   _____

3. Joseph is taking a keyboarding class.   _____

Conversation B

4. Joseph needs to use a computer at work.   _____

5. The computer lab is next door to Joseph's classroom.   _____

6. Mr. Stephens is the lab instructor.   _____

Conversation C

7. Joseph needs to register for a keyboarding class.   _____

8. Mrs. Smith works in the computer lab.   _____

9. Joseph needs to register next month.   _____

Listen again. Check your answers.

3 After you listen

Talk with a partner. Ask and answer the questions.

1. What are some important skills?

2. What new skills do you want to learn?

☑ Listen for and identify a student's future plans at school   **UNIT 2**   **19**

LESSON B What do you want to do?

1 Grammar focus: *want* and *need* + *to* + verb

Questions

What	do	you	**want** to do?
	does	he	
	do	they	

Answers

I	**want**	to learn English.
He	**wants**	
They	**want**	

Questions

What	**do**	you	**need** to do?
	does	she	
	do	they	

Answers

I	**need**	to take an English class.
She	**needs**	
They	**need**	

Turn to page 142 for a complete grammar chart.

> **CULTURE** NOTE
>
> The GED (General Equivalency Diploma) is a certificate. It is equal to a high school diploma.

2 Practice

A Write. Complete the conversations.

1. **A** What do you want to do now?

   B I ___*want to get*___ my GED.
   (want / get)

2. **A** What do you need to do?

   B I _____ a GED class.
   (need / take)

3. **A** What does Sandra want to do this year?

   B She _____ about computers.
   (want / learn)

4. **A** What does Ali want to do this year?

   B He _____ more money.
   (want / make)

5. **A** What does Celia need to do tonight?

   B She _____ her homework.
   (need / do)

6. **A** What do Sergio and Elena want to do next year?

   B They _____ citizens.
   (want / become)

Listen and repeat. Then practice with a partner.

CLASS CD1 TK 13

4 Picture dictionary Vocational courses

1. *home health care*

2. _____

3. _____

4. _____

5. _____

6. _____

7. _____

8. _____

9. _____

A Write the words in the picture dictionary. Then listen and repeat.

STUDENT TK 12
CLASS CD1 TK 16

computer networking	dental assisting	nail care
counseling	fitness training	physical therapy assisting
criminal justice	home health care	veterinary assisting

B Talk with a partner. Ask and answer questions.

Do you want to study home health care?
Yes, I do.

Do you want to study counseling?
No, I don't.

☑ Read about a goal and steps to take; use vocabulary for vocational courses **UNIT 2 25**

LESSON **E** Writing

1 Before you write

A Talk with a partner. Ask and answer the questions.

1. What are your goals this year?
2. What is your most important goal? Why?
3. What do you need to do to reach your goal?

B Read about Angela's goal.

My Goal for Next Year

I have a big goal. I want to help my children with their homework. There are three steps I need to take to reach my goal. First, I need to learn to speak, read, and write English well. Second, I need to volunteer in my children's school. Third, I need to talk with their teachers and learn more about their homework assignments. Maybe I'll be ready to help my children with their homework in a few months.

C Write. Complete the chart about Angela's goal.

Angela's goal
She wants to:
help her children with their homework
She needs to:
1. _____
2. _____
3. _____
She will probably reach her goal in:
_____

D **Read** Donald's chart. Talk with a partner. Ask and answer the questions.

1. What does Donald want to do?
2. What does he need to do first?
3. What does he need to do second?
4. What does he need to do third?
5. When will he probably reach his goal?

> **My goal** *Donald*
>
> **I want to:**
>
> get a job as a security guard
>
> **I need to:**
>
> 1. take courses in criminal justice
> 2. get a training certificate
> 3. look for jobs in the newspaper and online
>
> **I will probably reach my goal in:**
>
> one or two years

E **Write.** Complete the chart about your goal.

> **My goal**
>
> **I want to:**
>
> _____
>
> **I need to:**
>
> 1. _____
> 2. _____
> 3. _____
>
> **I will probably reach my goal in:**
>
> _____

2 Write

Write a paragraph about your goal. Write about the steps you need to take. Use Exercises 1B, 1C, 1D, and 1E to help you.

> Begin sentences with words like *First*, *Second*, and *Third* to organize your ideas.

3 After you write

A **Read** your paragraph to a partner.

B **Check** your partner's paragraph.

- What is your partner's goal?
- What are the three steps?
- Did your partner use the words *First*, *Second*, and *Third*?

LESSON **F** Another view

COURSE CATALOG

General Equivalency Diploma (GED)

Do you want to get your GED? Then you need to practice your reading, writing, and math skills. Classes are in English or Spanish. No fee.

Instructor: Mr. Chen (English)
               Ms. Lopez (Spanish)
Days/Times: Mon, Wed 6:00 p.m.–8:00 p.m.

Media Repair

This class will teach you how to repair various types of media such as MP3 players, DVD players, and TVs. You will also learn about opening your own repair shop. Fee: $85

Instructor: Mr. Stern

Days/Times: Mon, Tues 6:00 p.m.–8:00 p.m.

Introduction to Computers

This class is for adults who want to learn about computers and the Internet. You will learn about keyboarding, e-mail, and computer jobs. Fee: $75

Instructor: Mrs. Gates

Days/Times: Mon, Wed 7:00 p.m.–9:00 p.m.

Citizenship

Do you want to be an American citizen? First, you need to learn about American history and civics. This class will prepare you for the U.S. citizenship test. Requirements: Legal resident. No fee.

Instructor: Ms. Cuevas

Days/Times: Thurs 7:00 p.m.–9:00 p.m.

A **Read** the questions. Look at the course catalog. Fill in the answer.

1. How much will the GED class cost?
   - Ⓐ $35
   - Ⓑ $75
   - Ⓒ $85
   - Ⓓ free

2. When is the computer class?
   - Ⓐ Monday and Tuesday
   - Ⓑ Monday and Wednesday
   - Ⓒ Tuesday and Thursday
   - Ⓓ Wednesday and Friday

3. Who will teach Media Repair?
   - Ⓐ Mr. Stern
   - Ⓑ Ms. Cuevas
   - Ⓒ Mrs. Gates
   - Ⓓ Mr. Chen

4. Which class is in English or Spanish?
   - Ⓐ Citizenship
   - Ⓑ GED
   - Ⓒ Introduction to Computers
   - Ⓓ Media Repair

B **Talk** with a partner. Ask and answer the questions.

1. What do you want to learn about this year?
2. What classes will you probably take?

2 Grammar connections: the future with *be going to*, *will*, and the present continuous

There are three ways to talk about future events.	
be going to	Martin **is going to make** dinner after class.
will	He **will make** dinner after class.
the present continuous	He**'s making** dinner after class.

A **Work in a group.** Ask questions and complete the chart.

A What *are* you *going to do* after class?

B I*'m going* to make dinner.

A What *are* you *doing* tomorrow?

B I*'m going* shopping.

	(name)	(name)
1. What are you going to do after class?		
2. What are you doing tomorrow?		
3. What time will you get up tomorrow?		
4. What are you going to wear tomorrow?		
5. What are you doing next weekend?		
6. What class will you take next semester?		
7. Where will you go on your next vacation?		

B **Share** your group's information with the class.

Martin is going to make dinner after class. He's going shopping tomorrow. He . . .

3 Wrap up

Complete the **Self-assessment** on page 136.

Review

1 Listening

Read the questions. Then listen and circle the answers.

CLASS CD1 TK 17

1. How old is Fernando?
   a. 25
   b. 35 *(circled)*

2. What color is his hair?
   a. brown
   b. black

3. Where does he go in the morning?
   a. to school
   b. to work

4. What does he do at Green's Grocery Store?
   a. He's a cashier.
   b. He's a computer technician.

5. When does Fernando play soccer?
   a. on Saturday
   b. on Sunday

6. What does Fernando want to study?
   a. computer repair
   b. computer technology

Talk with a partner. Ask and answer the questions. Use complete sentences.

2 Grammar

A Write. Complete the story.

An Important Day

Tan Nguyen ___*is*___ 45 years old. He is a home health assistant.
        1. be

He _____ a nurse. He _____ from 8:00 a.m. to
   2. want / be   3. work

4:00 p.m., but today he _____ . This afternoon, he and his
              4. not / work

wife _____ United States citizens. Every day at work, Tan
    5. become

_____ a uniform. Today he _____ a new blue
   6. wear   7. wear

suit, a white shirt, and a red and white striped tie. Tan is very excited.

B Write. Look at the answers. Write the questions.

1. **A** How old _____*is Tan*_____?
   B Tan is 45 years old.

2. **A** What _____?
   B He is a home health assistant.

3. **A** When _____?
   B He usually works from 8:00 a.m. to 4:00 p.m.

4. **A** What _____?
   B Today he is wearing a blue suit, a white shirt, and a striped tie.

Talk with a partner. Ask and answer the questions.

3 Pronunciation: strong syllables

CLASS CD1 TK 18

A Listen to the syllables in these words.

•   •   •

paper   restaurant   computer

CLASS CD1 TK 19

B Listen and repeat. Clap for each syllable. Clap loudly for the strong syllable.

● ●	● ●	● ● ●	● ● ●	● ● ● ●
necklace	cashier	medium	mechanic	television
keyboard	career	counselor	tomorrow	citizenship
bracelet	repair	uniform	computer	
sweater	achieve	manager	eraser	
jacket		citizen		

Talk with a partner. Take turns. Say each word. Your partner claps for each syllable.

CLASS CD1 TK 20

C Listen for the strong syllable in each word. Put a dot over the strong syllable.

1. instrúctor   4. dictionary   7. management

2. partner   5. business   8. relax

3. enroll   6. sunglasses   9. important

D Write eight words from Units 1 and 2. Put a dot over the strong syllable in each word.

1.	5.
2.	6.
3.	7.
4.	8.

Talk with a partner. Read the words.

LESSON A
Listening

1 Before you listen

A Look at the picture. What do you see?

B Point to: a broken-down car • smoke • groceries • a trunk
a worried woman • an overheated engine • a hood

C Look at the people. What happened?

Rosa

Tomás

Laura

Unit Goals
Describe events in chronological order
Write a journal entry about past activities
Interpret information about cell phone calling plans

2 Listen

STUDENT TK 13
CLASS CD1 TK 21

A Listen. Who is Rosa talking to? Write the letter of the conversation.

1. _____

2. _____

3. _____

B Listen again. Write *T* (true) or *F* (false).

STUDENT TK 13
CLASS CD1 TK 21

Conversation A

1. Rosa calls her boss.   *F*
2. Rosa's husband is going to come from work.   _____
3. Rosa knows the problem with the car.   _____

Conversation B

4. Mike works at a coffee shop.   _____
5. Mike will pick up the car this afternoon.   _____
6. Mike will pick up Rosa and her children.   _____

Conversation C

7. Ling needs a ride to school tonight.   _____
8. Rosa usually leaves her house at 7:00.   _____
9. Ling will pick up Rosa at 8:00.   _____

Listen again. Check your answers.

3 After you listen

Talk with a partner. Ask and answer the questions.

1. Did you ever ask a friend for help? If yes, what happened?
2. Did a friend or family member ever ask you for help? If yes, what happened?

LESSON **B** What did you do last weekend?

1 Grammar focus: simple past with regular and irregular verbs

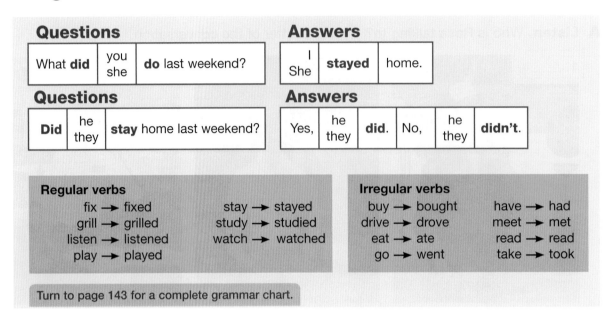

Questions

What **did**	you she	**do** last weekend?

Answers

	I She	**stayed**	home.

Questions

Did	he they	**stay** home last weekend?

Answers

Yes,	he they	**did**.	No,	he they	**didn't**.

Regular verbs

fix → fixed   stay → stayed
grill → grilled   study → studied
listen → listened   watch → watched
play → played

Irregular verbs

buy → bought   have → had
drive → drove   meet → met
eat → ate   read → read
go → went   take → took

Turn to page 143 for a complete grammar chart.

2 Practice

A Write. Complete the conversations. Use the simple past.

1. **A** What did Dahlia and her friends do on Sunday?

   B They ___*grilled*___ hamburgers.
   (grill)

2. **A** What did the children do on Thursday?

   B They _____ a walk in the park.
   (take)

3. **A** What did your family do last weekend?

   B We _____ to the beach.
   (drive)

4. **A** What did Sarah do Monday night?

   B She _____ to the movies.
   (go)

5. **A** What did Nikos do Saturday morning?

   B He _____ the car.
   (fix)

6. **A** What did Carlos do Wednesday morning?

   B He _____ groceries.
   (buy)

Listen and repeat. Then practice with a partner.

CLASS CD1 TK 22

34 UNIT 3

B Talk with a partner. Change the **bold** words and make conversations.

> A What did **Alicia** do last weekend?
> B **She went shopping** and **read a book**.

Alicia	John	Lisa and Sam
go shopping	eat in a restaurant	have a picnic
read a book	listen to music	play soccer

C Talk with a partner. Change the **bold** words and make conversations. Look at the pictures in Exercise 2B.

> A Did **Alicia go shopping** last weekend?
> B **Yes, she did.**

> A Did John **play soccer** last weekend?
> B **No, he didn't. He listened to music.**

1. Alicia / go shopping
2. John / play soccer
3. Sam and Lisa / read a book
4. John / eat in a restaurant
5. Alicia / have a picnic
6. Sam and Lisa / play soccer

3 Communicate

Talk with your classmates. Ask and answer questions about last weekend.

> A Karen, did you go to the beach last weekend?
> B No, I didn't. I stayed home.

> A Marco, what did you do last weekend?
> B I studied for a test.

☑ Use the simple past with regular and irregular verbs **UNIT 3 35**

LESSON C When do you usually play soccer?

1 Grammar focus: simple present vs. simple past

Simple present

When What time	**do** **does** **do**	you he they	usually **play** soccer?

I He They	usually	**play** soccer **plays** soccer **play** soccer	on Sunday. at 10:00.

Simple past

When What time	**did**	you she they	**play** soccer yesterday?

I She They	**played** soccer	after lunch. at noon.

> Turn to pages 141 and 143 for complete grammar charts.

2 Practice

A Write. Complete the conversations. Use the simple present or the simple past.

1. **A** When does Sharon usually meet her friends?
   B She usually ___*meets*___ her friends after work.
   A When did Sharon meet her friends yesterday?
   B Yesterday, she ___*met*___ them at noon for lunch.

2. **A** What time do Roberto and Selma usually eat dinner?
   B They usually _____ dinner at 7:00.
   A When did they eat dinner last night?
   B They _____ dinner at 8:00.

3. **A** When do Irma and Ron usually study?
   B They usually _____ on Saturday.
   A When did they study last weekend?
   B They _____ on Friday night.

4. **A** When do you usually watch movies?
   B I usually _____ movies after dinner.
   A What time did you watch a movie last night?
   B I _____ a movie at 6:00.

Listen and repeat. Then practice with a partner.

CLASS CD1 TK 23

B **Talk** with a partner. Change the **bold** words and make conversations.

> **A** When does Karim usually **go to the gym**?
> **B** He usually **goes to the gym** at **7:00 a.m.**

1. go to the gym / 7:00 a.m.   3. eat lunch / 1:00 p.m.
2. take a shower / 9:00 a.m.   4. go to work / 2:00 p.m.

C **Talk** with a partner. Change the **bold** words and make conversations.

> **A** When did Maria **get up** last Saturday?
> **B** She **got up** at **8:00 a.m.**

1. get up / 8:00 a.m.   4. clean her apartment / 6:00 p.m.
2. go shopping / 10:00 a.m.   5. go to the movies / 7:30 p.m.
3. go to her citizenship class / 1:00 p.m. 6. get home / 10:00 p.m.

3 Communicate

Talk with your classmates. Ask and answer questions about daily activities.

When do you usually get up?

I usually get up at 7:00 a.m.

When did you get up this morning?

I got up at 7:30 a.m.

☑ Use the simple present and simple past   **UNIT 3   37**

LESSON **D** Reading

1 Before you read

Look at the picture. Answer the questions.

1. Who is the woman?
2. What is she thinking about?

2 Read

Read Rosa's journal. Listen and read again.

STUDENT TK 14
CLASS CD1 TK 24

Thursday, June 20th

    Today was a bad day! On Thursday, my children and I usually go to the park for a picnic, but today we had a problem. We drove to the store to buy groceries, and then the car broke down. I checked the engine, and there was a lot of smoke. I think the engine overheated. Luckily, I had my cell phone! First, I called my husband at work. He left early, picked us up, and took us home. Next, I called the mechanic. Finally, I called Ling and asked for a ride to school tonight. In the end, we didn't go to the park because it was too late. Instead, we had a picnic in our backyard. Then, Ling drove me to school.

> Look for these words: *First*, *Next*, *Finally*. They tell the order of events.

3 After you read

A Write. Answer the questions about Rosa's day. Write complete sentences.

1. Where do Rosa and her children go on Thursday? *They go to the park.*

2. Why did they go to the store? _____

3. Who did Rosa call first? _____

4. Who picked up Rosa and the children? _____

5. What did Ling do? _____

B Number the sentences in the correct order.

_____ Ling drove Rosa to school.

_____ Rosa called her husband at work.

_____ Rosa's husband took them home.

_*1*_ Rosa went to the store.

_____ The car broke down.

4 Picture dictionary Daily activities

1. _make lunch_

2. _____

3. _____

4. _____

5. _____

6. _____

7. _____

8. _____

9. _____

STUDENT TK 15
CLASS CD1 TK 25

A Write the words in the picture dictionary. Then listen and repeat.

do homework	get dressed	make the bed
do the dishes	get up	take a bath
do the laundry	make lunch	take a nap

B Talk with a partner. Change the **bold** words and make conversations.

> A Did you **do the laundry** yesterday?
> B Yes, I did.

> A Did you **make the bed** this morning?
> B No, I didn't. **I got up late**.

☑ Read a journal entry about past events; use vocabulary for daily activities   **UNIT 3   39**

LESSON **E** Writing

1 Before you write

A **Write.** Think about a day last week. Draw three pictures about that day. Write a sentence about each picture. Use the simple past.

1.	2.	3.

1. _____
2. _____
3. _____

Talk with a partner. Share your pictures and sentences.

B **Read** Tina's journal.

Tuesday, September 1

Last Saturday, I went shopping. I bought five bags of food. I put the groceries in the trunk of my car. Then, I drove home. When I got home, I didn't have my purse. It wasn't in the car, and it wasn't in the trunk. First, I drove back to the store. Next, I looked for my purse outside by the shopping carts, but I didn't find it. Finally, I went inside and asked the manager about my purse. He looked and found my purse in the Lost and Found. I was very happy. In the end, it was a good day.

> **CULTURE** NOTE
>
> Many places have a *Lost and Found*. Go there to find lost things.

C **Write.** Answer the questions about Tina's day. Write complete sentences.

1. When did Tina go shopping? *She went shopping last Saturday.* _____
2. Where did she put the groceries? _____
3. Where did she first look for her purse? _____
4. Where was her purse? _____

D **Write** Read the sentences. Write *First*, *Next*, or *Finally* on the correct line.

> Use a comma after sequence words.
> **First,** *I washed the dirty clothes.*

1. Last Saturday, I did the laundry.

   _____, I dried the clothes in the dryer.

   _____, I folded the clean clothes.

   ____*First*____, I washed the dirty clothes.

2. Last night, I stayed home.

   _____, I washed the dishes.

   _____, I cooked dinner.

   _____, I went to bed.

3. Last Thursday, my family had a picnic.

   _____, we ate breakfast.

   _____, we woke up early.

   _____, we went to the park.

E **Write** the sentences from Exercise 1D in the correct order.

1. *Last Saturday, I did the laundry. First, I washed the dirty clothes. Next, ...*

   _____

   _____

2. _____

   _____

   _____

3. _____

   _____

   _____

2 Write

Write a journal entry about a day in your life. Use Exercises 1A, 1B, and 1E to help you.

3 After you write

A **Read** your journal entry to a partner.

B **Check** your partner's journal entry.

- What kind of day did your partner have?
- What happened first?
- Are there commas after the sequence words (*First*, *Next*, *Finally*)?

LESSON F Another view

1 Life-skills reading

E-Z Cell Phone Calling Plans – Monthly Rates

Plan Name	Shared anytime minutes	Talk, Text, and Data	Talk and Text	Cost for each additional minute
Plan A	700	$ 99.99	$ 69.99	$ .45
Plan B	1,400	$ 119.99	$ 89.99	$ .40
Plan C	2,000	$ 129.99	$ 99.99	$ .35
Plan D	Unlimited	$ 149.99	$ 119.99	None

A Read the questions. Look at the cell phone calling plans. Fill in the answer.

1. Which plan costs $129.99 per month?
   - (A) Plan A
   - (B) Plan B
   - (C) Plan C
   - (D) Plan D

2. How much is each additional minute with Plan B?
   - (A) $0.35
   - (B) $0.40
   - (C) $0.45
   - (D) No charge

3. How much is Plan A for talking and texting only?
   - (A) $69.99
   - (B) $89.99
   - (C) $99.99
   - (D) $119.99

4. How many minutes come with Plan C?
   - (A) 700
   - (B) 1,400
   - (C) 2,000
   - (D) unlimited

B Talk with a partner. Ask and answer the questions.

1. Do you have a cell phone? If so, what kind of cell phone plan do you have?
2. When do you usually call your friends? What do you talk about?
3. Sue usually talks and texts on the phone about 1,600 minutes a month. Which plan should she choose?

2 Grammar connections: *make* and *do*; *play* and *go*

Use *do* to talk about most chores. Exception: *make the bed*	Did you **do the dishes**? We **did the laundry** after school.
Use *make* for activities when you create or build something.	My mother **made a dress.** I **made lunch**. / I **made tacos**.
Use *play* with many sports, games, and musical instruments.	My brother **plays baseball** well. I **play board games** with my friends. Jenna **plays the guitar**.
Use *go* + verb + *ing* for activities.	I usually **go jogging** in the morning. Do you **go shopping** on the weekends?

A Work with a partner. Write the words under the correct verb.

biking	chores	football	jewelry
breakfast	dancing	hiking	laundry
cards	dinner	homework	piano
chess	fishing	housework	pizza

Do	Make	Play	Go
			biking

B Work in a group. Choose a word from 2A. Act out the activity in front of your group. Your classmates guess.

A Are you playing chess?

B No, I'm not.

C Are you playing the piano?

B Yes, I am.

3 Wrap up

Complete the **Self-assessment** on page 137.

LESSON **A**
Listening

1 **Before you listen**

A Look at the picture. What do you see?

B Point to: crutches • an injured hand • broken bones
a sprained ankle • an inhaler • an X-ray • a painful knee

C Where are these people? What happened to them?

Hamid

No Cell Phones

Unit Goals
Read warning labels
Complete an accident report form
Interpret medicine labels

2 Listen

A **Listen.** Who is Hamid talking to? Write the letter of the conversation.

STUDENT TK 16
CLASS CD1 TK 26

1. ____

2. ____

ACE Construction

3. ____

B **Listen again.** Write *T* (true) or *F* (false).

STUDENT TK 16
CLASS CD1 TK 26

Conversation A

1. Hamid had an accident at home.   *F*

2. Hamid fell off a ladder.   ____

3. Hamid will pick up his children.   ____

Conversation B

4. Hamid had to get an X-ray.   ____

5. Chris can't drive Hamid home.   ____

6. The hospital is on 53rd Street.   ____

Conversation C

7. Mr. Jackson will fill out an accident report.   ____

8. Hamid has to finish the paint job.   ____

9. Hamid will stay home tomorrow.   ____

Listen again. Check your answers.

3 After you listen

Talk with a partner. Ask and answer the questions.

1. What jobs are dangerous? Why?

2. Did you ever have an accident at work? What happened?

3. Did you ever have an accident at home? What happened?

☑ Listen for and identify information about an accident   **UNIT 4**   **45**

LESSON **B** You should go to the hospital.

1 Grammar focus: *should*

Questions			
What	**should**	I	do?
		she	
		they	

Answers		
You	**should**	go to the hospital.
She		
They		

You	**shouldn't**	work.
She		
They		

Turn to page 144 for a complete grammar chart.

shouldn't = should not

2 Practice

A Write. Complete the conversations. Use *should* or *shouldn't.*

1. **A** Ken's eyes hurt. What ___*should*___ he do?

   B He should rest. He ___*shouldn't*___ read right now.

2. **A** They have stomachaches. What _____ they do?

   B They _____ eat. They _____ take some medicine.

3. **A** My tooth hurts. What _____ I do?

   B You _____ see a dentist.

4. **A** Mia has a headache. What _____ she do?

   B She _____ take some aspirin.

5. **A** I hurt my leg. What _____ I do?

   B You _____ get an X-ray.

   You _____ walk.

6. **A** I have a bottle of medicine.

   What _____ I do?

   B You _____ read the label.

   You shouldn't keep it in a hot place.

Listen and repeat. Then practice with a partner.

CLASS CD1 TK 27

B **Look** at the pictures of Alan. He is gardening. It's very hot. Check (✓) the things he should do.

☐ Drink lots of water.

☐ Wear heavy clothes.

☐ Take a break.

☐ Use a wet towel.

☐ Stay in the sun.

☐ Stay in the shade.

Talk with a partner. Look at the pictures again. Change the **bold** words and make conversations.

A Alan doesn't feel well. What should he do?
B He should **drink lots of water**. He shouldn't **stay in the sun**.
A OK. I'll tell him.

> **USEFUL** LANGUAGE
>
> *I'll tell him.*
> *I'll let him know.*

3 Communicate

Talk in a group. Read the problems. Give advice.

1. Teresa's wrist is very sore. What should she do?

2. Ed is very hot. He doesn't feel well. What should he do?

3. Susana fell off her chair. What should her mother do?

LESSON **C** You have to see a doctor.

1 Grammar focus: *have to* + verb

Questions

What	do	I	have to do?
	does	he	
	do	they	

Answers

You	have to	see a doctor.
He	has to	
They	have to	

Turn to page 142 for a complete grammar chart.

2 Practice

A Write. Complete the conversations. Use *have to* or *has to*.

1. **A** Elian hurt his leg.

   B He _____*has to*_____ get an X-ray.

2. **A** Kathy and Tom have asthma.

   B They _____ take their medicine.

3. **A** My son broke his arm.

   B You _____ take him to
   the hospital.

4. **A** Marcia has a sprained ankle.

   B She _____ get a pair of crutches.

5. **A** Nick and Tony had an accident at work.

   B They _____ fill out an
   accident report.

6. **A** Pam hurt her back.

   B She _____ go home early.

Listen and repeat. Then practice with a partner.

CLASS CD1 TK 28

B **Talk** with a partner. Change the **bold** words and make conversations.

A Here's your prescription. You have to **keep** this medicine **in the refrigerator**.
B OK. I have to **keep** this medicine **in the refrigerator**.
A Yes. Call me if you have any questions.

USEFUL LANGUAGE

OK.
I understand.
Yes, I see.

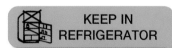
KEEP IN REFRIGERATOR

TAKE IN THE MORNING

SHAKE WELL

TAKE WITH FOOD

KEEP OUT OF REACH OF CHILDREN

CULTURE NOTE

Warning labels on medicine say what you should and shouldn't do.

3 Communicate

Talk with a partner. What happened to these people? What do they have to do?

1.

2.

3.

She burned her hand.

She has to see a doctor.

LESSON **D** Reading

1 Before you read

Look at the picture. Answer the questions.

1. Who is the man?
2. What is he doing?
3. What should he do?

2 Read

Read the warning label. Listen and read again.

STUDENT TK 17
CLASS CD1 TK 29

WARNING: PREVENT ACCIDENTS. READ BEFORE USING!

- Face the ladder when climbing up and down.
- Don't carry a lot of equipment while climbing a ladder – wear a tool belt.
- Never stand on the shelf of the ladder – stand on the steps.
- Never stand on the top step of a ladder.
- Be safe! Always read and follow the safety stickers.

Lists often begin with a number or bullet (•). Each numbered or bulleted item is a new idea.

3 After you read

A Write. Complete the sentences. Use *should* or *shouldn't*.

1. You ___*shouldn't*___ carry a lot of equipment while climbing a ladder.
2. You _____ read and follow the safety stickers.
3. You _____ face the ladder when climbing up or down.
4. You _____ stand on the shelf of the ladder.

B Write. Complete the paragraph.

> **CULTURE** NOTE
>
> In emergencies, dial 911 for help.

| accidents | ladder | safe | safety | tool belt |

Be Careful in the Workplace!

Don't have ___*accidents*___ at work. Always read the _____ stickers on your
          1   2

tools and equipment. When you climb a _____, wear a _____.
                                          3   4

When you carry heavy items, ask someone to help you. We want our workers to be

_____ and healthy.
   5

4 Picture dictionary Health problems

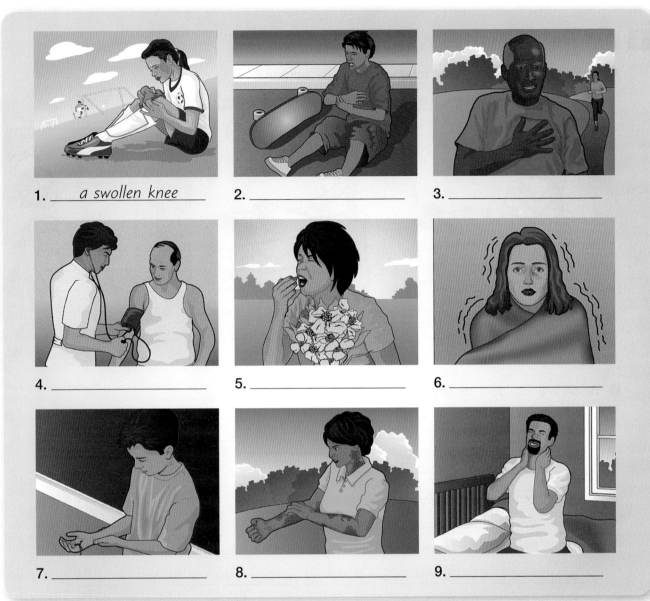

1. _a swollen knee_
2. _____
3. _____

4. _____
5. _____
6. _____

7. _____
8. _____
9. _____

STUDENT TK 18
CLASS CD1 TK 30

A Write the words in the picture dictionary. Then listen and repeat.

allergies	chills	a sprained wrist
a bad cut	high blood pressure	a stiff neck
chest pains	a rash	a swollen knee

B Talk with a partner. Change the **bold** words and make conversations.

A **She** has **a swollen knee**. What should **she** do?
B **She** should **stay in bed and use ice**.

LESSON E Writing

1 Before you write

A **Talk** with a partner. What happened to this woman?

B **Read** the accident report.

ACCIDENT REPORT FORM

Employee name: _Komiko Yanaka_

Date of accident: _September 13, 2013_   Time: _9:00 p.m._

Type of injury: _cut foot_

How did the accident happen? _Last night, I was in the kitchen. Every night, I cut_
vegetables. Last night, the knife fell and cut my foot. I had to go to
the doctor.

Signature: _Komiko Yanaka_   Date: _9/14/13_

C **Write.** Answer the questions about the accident report.

1. Who had an accident? _Komiko Yanaka_
2. When did the accident happen? _____
3. What was the injury? _____
4. How did the injury happen? _____
5. When did she sign the form? _____

D Write. Work with a partner. Read the sentences. Number the sentences in the correct order.

1. Yesterday, I cut my foot.

   ____ It fell on my foot.

   ____ The knife fell.

   _1_ I was in the kitchen.

2. Yesterday, I sprained my ankle.

   ____ There was water on the floor.

   ____ I have to fill out an accident report.

   ____ I slipped.

3. Yesterday, I broke my leg.

   ____ I fell off the ladder.

   ____ I went to the hospital.

   ____ I was at the top of a ladder.

4. Yesterday, I hurt my back.

   ____ I felt a terrible pain in my back.

   ____ I picked up a heavy box.

   ____ I have to see a doctor tomorrow.

2 Write

Complete the accident report form. Use your imagination or write about a real accident. Use Exercises 1B and 1D to help you.

ACCIDENT REPORT FORM

Employee name: _____

Date of accident: _____   Time: _____

Type of injury: _____

How did the accident happen? _____

_____

_____

_____

_____

Signature: _____   Date: _____

---

3 After you write

A Read your form to a partner.

B Check your partner's form.

- What was the injury?
- What was the date of the accident?
- Is there a signature on the form?

> Your signature on a form makes it official. For a signature, use cursive writing. Don't print.
>
> _Carl Stanley_
> ~~Carl Stanley~~

LESSON **F** Another view

1 Life-skills reading

Drug facts	
Active ingredient (in each tablet)	**Purpose**
Acetaminophen 325 mg	Pain reliever

Uses Temporary relief of minor aches and pains

Warnings
- Ask a doctor or pharmacist before use if you are taking a prescription drug.
- Ask a doctor before use if you have liver or kidney disease.
- When using this product, do not take more than directed.
- Can cause drowsiness.
- Keep out of reach of children.

Directions
- Adults and children 12 years and over: Take 2 tablets every 4 to 6 hours as needed. Do not take more than 8 tablets in 24 hours.
- Children under 12 years of age: Ask a doctor.

A Read the questions. Look at the medicine label. Fill in the answer.

1. Why should you take this medicine?
   - Ⓐ for drowsiness
   - Ⓑ for aches and pains
   - Ⓒ for kidney disease
   - Ⓓ for liver disease

2. How many tablets should children under 12 take at one time?
   - Ⓐ 2 tablets
   - Ⓑ 4 tablets
   - Ⓒ no tablets
   - Ⓓ none of the above

3. How many tablets should an adult take at one time?
   - Ⓐ 2 tablets
   - Ⓑ 4 tablets
   - Ⓒ 6 tablets
   - Ⓓ 8 tablets

4. How many tablets can an adult take in one day?
   - Ⓐ 8 tablets
   - Ⓑ 12 tablets
   - Ⓒ 24 tablets
   - Ⓓ none of the above

B Talk with a partner. Ask and answer the questions.

1. Your father has a headache. How many tablets should you give him?
2. Your son is four years old. Should you give him any tablets?
3. Jane has kidney disease. She wants to take a tablet. What does she have to do first?
4. Paul is taking a prescription drug. He wants to take this medicine. What should he do?

2 Grammar connections: *must, must not, have to, not have to*

must, have to = required	You **must take** this medicine three times a day. You **have to take** it three times a day.
must not = not allowed	You **must not drive** after you take it.
not have to = not necessary, but OK	You **don't have to take** it with food, but you can.

A **Work** with a partner. Write *have to / must*, *must not*, or *don't have to*.

- Take with plenty of water.
- Take one pill three times a day with or without food.

1. You ____*have to / must*____ take this medication with water.
   You also ____*must / have to*____ take it three times a day.
   You _____ take it with food.

- Take once a day with food.
- Do not drive after taking medication.
- Refrigerate medication.

2. You _____ take this medication once a
   day. You _____ drive after taking it. You
   _____ keep the medication in
   the refrigerator.

- Take when needed.
- Stay out of the sun.
- Do not give to children.

3. You _____ take this medication every day.
   You _____ be in the sun after taking it. You
   _____ give this medication to children.

- Take twice a day.
- Do not take with grapefruit juice.
- You may refrigerate medication.

4. You _____ take this medication twice a day.
   You _____ drink grapefruit juice when you
   take it. You _____ keep it in the refrigerator.

B **Work** with your partner. Have a conversation between a pharmacist and a customer. Use the labels in 2A. Take turns.

A Here's your medication. Remember, you have to take it with water.

B OK. Do I need to eat first?

A You don't have to eat first, but you can. You must take it three times a day.

3 Wrap up

Complete the **Self-assessment** on page 137.

☑ Scan a medicine label; contrast *must* and *must not* with *have to* and *not have to*   UNIT 4   **55**

Review

1 Listening

Read the questions. Then listen and circle the answers.

1. What does Trinh do?
   a. She's a nurse.
   b. She's a server.

2. Where does she work?
   a. at a hospital
   b. at a restaurant

3. Who became citizens on Friday?
   a. Trinh and her family
   b. Trinh and her husband

4. What did Trinh and her husband do at the beach?
   a. They took pictures.
   b. They took a nap.

5. When did they grill hamburgers?
   a. in the afternoon
   b. in the evening

6. What did they do at home?
   a. They read.
   b. They watched a movie.

Talk with a partner. Ask and answer the questions. Use complete sentences.

2 Grammar

A Write. Complete the story.

At the Doctor's Office

Yesterday, Manuel's wife Serena _____*took*_____ him to Dr. Scott's
                                        1. take
office. Dr. Scott _____ Manuel that he _____
                     2. tell   3. should / lose
weight. Manuel usually _____ a lot of fried food. He
                          4. eat
_____ a lot of coffee and soda. Dr. Scott said Manuel
   5. drink
_____ more fruit and vegetables and drink more water.
   6. should / eat
She said that Manuel _____ . Now he _____
                       7. should / exercise   8. have to
walk every day.

B Write. Look at the answers. Write the questions.

1. **A** *Where did Serena take Manuel?*
   B Serena took Manuel to Dr. Scott's office.

2. **A** What _____?
   B He usually eats fried food.

3. **A** What _____?
   B He should eat fruit and vegetables.

4. **A** What _____?
   B He has to exercise.

Talk with a partner. Ask and answer the questions.

3 Pronunciation: important words

A **Listen** to the important words in these sentences.

CLASS CD1 TK 32

Tina's **car** broke down.

Oscar has to take his **medicine**.

B **Listen and repeat.** Clap for each word. Clap loudly for the important word.

CLASS CD1 TK 33

1. His **wife** had to do it.
2. Van has a **headache**.
3. I played **soccer** last night.

4. They went to the **library** yesterday.
5. Eliza **works** in the afternoon.
6. **Sam** made breakfast.

C **Listen** for the important word in each sentence. Underline the important word.

CLASS CD1 TK 34

1. Ali cut his <u>arm</u>.
2. He went to the hospital.
3. His sister took him.

4. He saw the doctor.
5. He has to take some medicine.
6. He shouldn't carry heavy items.

Talk with a partner. Compare your answers.

D **Write** six sentences from Units 3 and 4. Then work with a partner. Underline the important words in your partner's sentences.

1.
2.
3.
4.
5.
6.

Talk with a partner. Read the sentences.

5 Around town

LESSON A
Listening

1 Before you listen

A Look at the picture. What do you see?

B Point to: an information desk • arrivals • departures
a track • a ticket booth • a suitcase • a waiting area

C Where are these people? What are they doing?

Unit Goals

Interpret information on train, bus, and airline schedules

Report frequency of activities

Write a letter about past travel

2 Listen

STUDENT TK 19
CLASS CD1 TK 35

A **Listen.** What is Binh talking about? Write the letter of the conversation.

1. _____

2. _____

3. _____

STUDENT TK 19
CLASS CD1 TK 35

B **Listen again.** Write *T* (true) or *F* (false).

Conversation A

1. Trains to Boston leave every hour. _____*T*_____

2. The next train to Boston will leave at 8:00. _____

3. The next train to Boston will leave from Track 1. _____

Conversation B

4. Trains to New York leave every hour. _____

5. The next train to New York will leave at 7:35. _____

6. Binh and his mother need to buy tickets. _____

Conversation C

7. Binh never travels by train. _____

8. It takes about two hours to drive to New York. _____

9. It takes two and a half hours to get to New York by train. _____

Listen again. Check your answers.

3 After you listen

Talk with a partner. How do you get to work? How do you get to school?

I go to work by bus, and I walk to school.

I take the train to work, and I drive to school.

☑ Listen for and identify departures and arrivals at a train station   **UNIT 5   59**

LESSON **B** How often? How long?

1 Grammar focus: *How often?* and *How long?*

Questions				Answers		
How often	do do does	trains you he	go to New York?	They I He	go go goes	**every 30 minutes.** **once a year.** **twice a month.**

Time phrases for frequency
every 30 minutes   every day   once a week   twice a month   three times a year

Question		Answers	
How long does it take	to go to New York?	It takes	**about two hours.** **around two hours.**

Time phrases for duration
about five minutes   a half hour   one hour   an hour and ten minutes   a long time

2 Practice

A Write. Circle the correct answers.

1. **A** How often does Binh go to New York?
   B 30 minutes. / ⟨Twice a month.⟩

2. **A** How long does it take to fly to Mexico?
   B A long time. / Once a month.

3. **A** How often do you study?
   B Three hours. / Twice a week.

4. **A** How long does it take to drive to Toronto?
   B Seven hours. / Once a day.

5. **A** How long does it take to walk to school?
   B Twice a week. / 20 minutes.

6. **A** How often does Sandra cook dinner?
   B Two hours. / Three times a week.

7. **A** How often does the bus go to Springfield?
   B Once a day. / A long time.

8. **A** How often do they go on vacation?
   B A long time. / Once a year.

9. **A** How long does it take to drive to the airport?
   B One hour. / Twice a year.

10. **A** How long does it take to walk to the library?
    B Every 30 minutes. / 25 minutes.

Listen and repeat. Then practice with a partner.

CLASS CD1 TK 36

B **Read** the bus schedule. Where does the bus go?

US Bus Schedule

Springfield to New York City		
Departs	Arrives	Duration
6:30 a.m.	9:00 a.m.	2h 30m
11:00 a.m.	1:30 p.m.	2h 30m
2:00 p.m.	4:30 p.m.	2h 30m
6:30 p.m.	9:00 p.m.	2h 30m

Springfield to Capital Airport		
Departs	Arrives	Duration
5:30 a.m.	6:50 a.m.	1h 20m
9:00 a.m.	10:20 a.m.	1h 20m
3:00 p.m.	4:20 p.m.	1h 20m
5:00 p.m.	6:20 p.m.	1h 20m
6:00 p.m.	7:20 p.m.	1h 20m

Springfield to Boston		
Departs	Arrives	Duration
8:00 a.m.	4:15 p.m.	8h 15m
9:30 a.m.	5:45 p.m.	8h 15m
11:00 a.m.	7:15 p.m.	8h 15m

Springfield to Washington, D.C.		
Departs	Arrives	Duration
7:45 a.m.	11:15 a.m.	3h 30m
9:45 a.m.	1:15 p.m.	3h 30m
11:00 a.m.	2:30 p.m.	3h 30m
1:00 p.m.	4:30 p.m.	3h 30m

h = hour   m = minute

C **Talk** with a partner. Change the **bold** words and make conversations.

A Excuse me. How often do buses go to **New York City**?
B They go **four** times a day.
A How long does it take to get there?
B It takes about **two and a half hours**.

USEFUL LANGUAGE

two and a half hours =
two hours and 30 minutes

a half hour = half an hour
= 30 minutes

an hour and a half =
one hour and 30 minutes

1. New York City   2. Boston   3. Washington, D.C.   4. the airport

3 Communicate

Talk with a partner. Ask questions. Complete the chart.

A How often do you walk to school?
B I walk to school every day. **OR**
I don't walk to school. I take a bus.

A How long does it take?
B It takes about half an hour.

	How often?	How long?
walk to school	*every day*	*half an hour*
take the bus to work		
drive to the store		
fly to another country		

LESSON C She often walks to school.

1 Grammar focus: adverbs of frequency

Statements

She	often sometimes rarely never	walks to school.

She is	always usually rarely never	late for class.

Adverbs of frequency

always	100% frequency
usually / often	
sometimes	
hardly ever / rarely	
never	0%

2 Practice

A Write. Use adverbs of frequency and make new sentences.

1. Teresa drives to work in the morning.

   Teresa always drives to work in the morning.
   (always)

2. She is late.

   _____
   (rarely)

3. Her husband walks to work.

   _____
   (usually)

4. He takes a taxi.

   _____
   (sometimes)

5. He drives.

   _____
   (never)

6. Their daughter rides her bike to school.

   _____
   (always)

7. She is tired in the morning.

   _____
   (often)

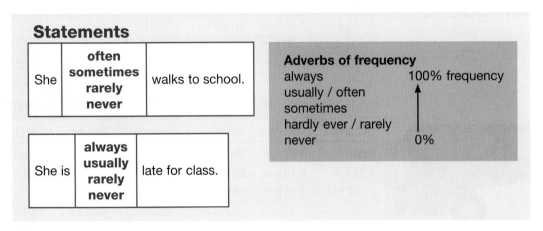

Listen and repeat. Check your answers.

CLASS CD1 TK 37

B **Talk** with a partner. Change the **bold** words and make conversations.

John		Never	Hardly ever	Usually	Always
	1. walks to school	✓			
	2. drives to school				✓
	3. is tired in the morning		✓		
	4. is hungry around 11:00 a.m.			✓	

Sunita		Never	Sometimes	Often	Always
	1. walks to school			✓	
	2. drives to school		✓		
	3. is tired in the morning				✓
	4. is hungry around 11:00 a.m.	✓			

A John **never walks to school**.
How about Sunita?
B She **often walks to school**.

USEFUL LANGUAGE

How about . . . ?
What about . . . ?

3 Communicate

A **Write.** Complete the sentences about yourself.

1. I am usually ___*hungry*___ around 11:00. I always ___*eat lunch*___ after class.
2. I am often _____ on Saturday.
3. I usually _____ during the summer.
4. I am never _____ in the afternoon.
5. I sometimes _____ late at night.
6. I always _____ on the weekend.
7. I rarely _____ in the morning.
8. I never _____ during the week.

B **Talk** with a partner. Use your answers from Exercise 3A.

I always eat lunch after class. What about you?

I always go to work after class.

UNIT 5

LESSON **D** Reading

1 Before you read

Look at the picture. Answer the questions.

1. Who do you see in the picture?
2. Where is she?
3. What is she doing?

Arrivals

2 Read

STUDENT TK 20
CLASS CD1 TK 38

Read the letter. Listen and read again.

Dear Layla,

Right now, my mother is visiting me here in Philadelphia.
I rarely see her because she comes to Philadelphia only once
a year. She usually stays for one month. Here is a photo of
my mother at the airport last week. She was happy to see me!
This year, I want to take my mother to New York City.
I want to show her the Statue of Liberty and Central Park.
It takes about one and a half hours to get to New York
by train. We are excited about our trip. Can you meet
us there? Let me know.

Your friend,
Binh

Capital letters can
show you the names
of cities or places.
New **Y**ork **C**ity
Statue of **L**iberty

3 After you read

Write. Correct the sentences.

1. Binh's mother comes to Philadelphia three times a year.

   Binh's mother comes to Philadelphia once a year.

2. Binh often sees his mother.

   _____

3. Binh wants to take his mother to Los Angeles.

   _____

4. Binh wants to show his mother the White House.

   _____

5. It takes two hours to get from Philadelphia to New York by train.

   _____

4 Picture dictionary Travel activities

1. _write postcards_

2. _____

3. _____

4. _____

5. _____

6. _____

7. _____

8. _____

9. _____

STUDENT TK 21
CLASS CD1 TK 39

A Write the words in the picture dictionary. Then listen and repeat.

buy souvenirs	go swimming	take a suitcase
go shopping	stay at a hotel	take pictures
go sightseeing	stay with relatives	write postcards

B Talk with a partner. Change the **bold** words and make conversations.

A Do you **write postcards** on a trip?

B Yes, I do. I always **write postcards**.

A Do you **stay at a hotel** on a trip?

B No, I don't. I never **stay at a hotel**.

☑ Read a letter about a visit; use vocabulary for travel activities **UNIT 5** **65**

LESSON **E** Writing

1 Before you write

A **Talk** with a partner. Ask and answer the questions.

1. When was your last trip?
2. Where did you go?
3. What did you do there?

B **Read** the letter from Alicia.

Willis Tower,
110 stories high

Millennium Park

Dear Margarita,

   How are you? I just got back from a trip to Chicago. I went to visit my cousin, Isaac. Isaac lives in a suburb about one hour from Chicago called Aurora. I always go to visit him once a year. It usually takes three hours to get there from Boston by plane.

   This year we spent three days in the city of Chicago. We went sightseeing. I saw the Willis Tower, the tallest building in the United States. We also saw a concert in Millennium Park. We went shopping, and I bought souvenirs. It was a fun trip! Hope you are well. Write soon!

Your friend,
Alicia

C **Write.** Answer the questions about Alicia's letter. Write complete sentences.

1. Where did Alicia go? _Alicia went to Chicago._
2. Who did she visit? _____
3. How often does she visit him? _____
4. How long does it usually take to get there? _____
   _____
5. What did she do there? _____
   _____
   _____

D Write. Answer the questions about yourself.

1. When was your last trip?

   _____

   _____

2. Where did you go?

   _____

   _____

3. How did you get there?

   _____

   _____

4. How often do you go there?

   _____

   _____

5. How long does it usually take to get there?

   _____

   _____

6. Who did you go with?

   _____

   _____

7. What did you do there?

   _____

   _____

> **USEFUL** LANGUAGE
>
> *How did you get there?*
> *By train.*   *By bus.*
> *By plane.*   *By car.*

2 Write

Write a letter to a friend about your last trip.
Use Exercises 1B and 1D to help you.

> Spell out hours and minutes
> from one to ten:
> *one hour and five minutes*
> Write all other times as numbers:
> *11 hours and 30 minutes*

3 After you write

A Read your letter to a partner.

B Check your partner's letter.

- Where did your partner go?
- How long does it usually take to get there?
- Did your partner write the hours and minutes correctly?

LESSON F Another view

Air American Flight Schedule

Flight	From	To	Departs	Arrives
Flight 885	Boston	New York	6:00 A.M.	7:35 A.M.
Flight 1005	Boston	New York	8:00 A.M.	9:09 A.M.
Flight 1007	Boston	New York	10:20 A.M.	11:30 A.M.
Flight 1009	Boston	New York	11:20 A.M.	12:35 P.M.
Flight 1015	Boston	New York	3:43 P.M.	5:00 P.M.
Flight 1017	Boston	New York	6:50 P.M.	8:18 P.M.

A Read the questions. Look at the airline schedule. Fill in the answer.

1. How long does it take to go to New York on Flight 1009?

    Ⓐ one hour

    Ⓑ one hour and five minutes

    Ⓒ one hour and ten minutes

    Ⓓ one hour and 15 minutes

2. How often do flights go from Boston to New York before 11:00 a.m.?

    Ⓐ once

    Ⓑ twice

    Ⓒ three times

    Ⓓ six times

3. How long does it take to go to New York on Flight 885?

    Ⓐ one hour and ten minutes

    Ⓑ one hour and 35 minutes

    Ⓒ an hour and a half

    Ⓓ two hours and ten minutes

4. How many flights arrive in New York after 11:00 a.m.?

    Ⓐ one

    Ⓑ two

    Ⓒ three

    Ⓓ four

B Talk with a partner. Ask and answer the questions.

1. How long does it take to go from Boston to New York on flight 1015?

2. How many flights go from Boston to New York in the morning?

3. What time does the first flight leave Boston to go to New York?

4. What time does the last flight leave Boston to go to New York?

2 Grammar connections: *into*, *out of*, *through*, and *toward*

Walk into
the museum.

Walk out of
the museum.

Walk through
the tunnel.

Walk toward
the desk.

A **Work with a partner.** Give directions to
a place in the museum. Your partner
guesses the place. Take turns.

> **A** Walk *into* the museum. Walk *toward* the Information Desk. Turn right.
> Then walk *through* Room A and *into* Room B. Next, walk *through* Tunnel 1.
> Where are you?
> **B** I'm in Room C.
> **A** That's right!

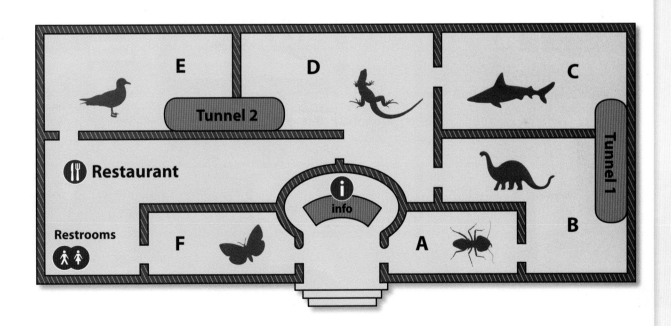

B **Work with your partner.** Give directions from
your classroom to a place in your school.
Use *into*, *out of*, *through*, and *toward*.

3 Wrap up

Complete the **Self-assessment** on page 138.

LESSON A
Listening

1 Before you listen

A Look at the picture. What do you see?

B Point to: a class picture • a family picture • a photo album
a baby picture • a graduation picture • a wedding picture

C Look at the people. What are they doing?

Olga

Victoria

2 Listen

STUDENT TK 22
CLASS CD2 TK 2

A **Listen.** What is Olga talking about? Write the letter of the conversation.

1. _____

2. _____

3. _____

STUDENT TK 22
CLASS CD2 TK 2

B **Listen again.** Write *T* (true) or *F* (false).

Conversation A

1. Olga moved into her apartment two months ago.   *T*

2. Olga got married in 1993.   _____

3. Victoria got married 30 years ago.   _____

Conversation B

4. Sergey is 14.   _____

5. Sergey started college in September.   _____

6. Natalya started college on Tuesday.   _____

Conversation C

7. Olga met her husband in Moscow.   _____

8. Olga moved to Russia about 14 years ago.   _____

9. Natalya was born in Russia.   _____

Listen again. Check your answers. Correct the false statements.

3 After you listen

Talk with a partner. Ask and answer the questions.

1. When do children start high school and college in countries you know?

2. At what age do people get married in countries you know?

3. When do people usually start their first jobs?

LESSON **B** When did you move here?

1 Grammar focus: *When* questions and simple past

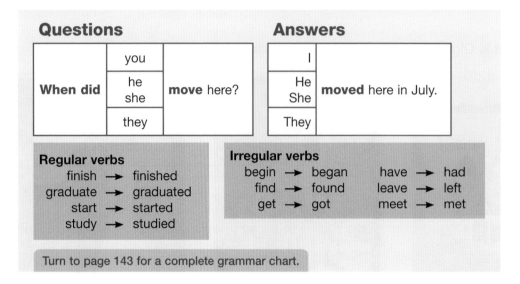

Questions			Answers		
When did	you / he she / they	**move** here?	I / He She / They	**moved** here in July.	

Regular verbs
finish → finished
graduate → graduated
start → started
study → studied

Irregular verbs
begin → began   have → had
find → found   leave → left
get → got   meet → met

Turn to page 143 for a complete grammar chart.

2 Practice

A Write. Complete the conversations. Use the simple past.

1. **A** When did Min leave South Korea?
   B She _____*left*_____ South Korea in 2004.
   A When did she move to New York?
   B She _____ to New York in 2006.

2. **A** When did Carlos start school?
   B He _____ school in September.
   A When did he graduate?
   B He _____ in June.

3. **A** When did Paul and Amy meet?
   B They _____ in 2009.
   A When did they get married?
   B They _____ married in 2012.

Listen and repeat. Then practice with a partner.

CLASS CD2 TK 3

B **Read** Kasem's and Nee's time lines.

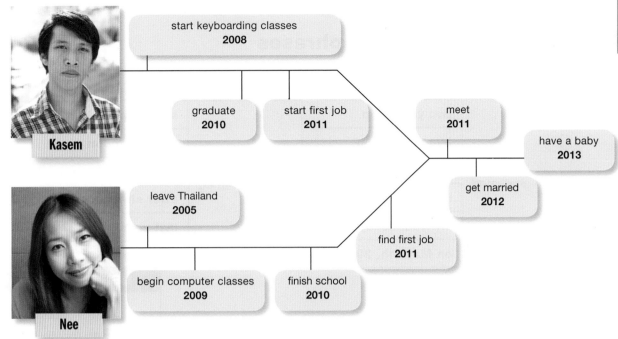

Talk with a partner. Change the **bold** words and make conversations.

> **A** When did **Kasem start keyboarding classes**?
> **B** **He started keyboarding classes** in **2008**.

1. Kasem / start keyboarding classes
2. Nee / begin computer classes
3. Kasem / graduate
4. Kasem and Nee / meet
5. Nee / find her first job
6. Kasem and Nee / have a baby
7. Nee / finish school
8. Kasem and Nee / get married
9. Nee / leave Thailand
10. Kasem / start his first job

3 Communicate

Talk with a partner. Complete the chart.

> **A** Ali, when did you start English classes?
> **B** I started English classes in 2010.

start English classes	*in 2010*
move to this country	
start your first job	

LESSON C He graduated two years ago.

1 Grammar focus: time phrases

Statements

He graduated		She got married	
	two years ago.		at 3:00 p.m.
	two weeks ago.		at 12:00 noon.
	in May.		before she came to the U.S.
	in 2009.		after she came to the U.S.
	on Wednesday.		last year.
	on May 4th, 2009.		this week.

USEFUL LANGUAGE

Use *at* with time.

Use *in* with months and years.

Use *on* with days and dates.

Use *ago* with phrases for periods of time.

Use *before* and *after* with a subject and verb.

2 Practice

A Write. Complete the conversations. Use *at*, *in*, *on*, or *ago*.

1. **A** When did Lou and Angela buy their new car?

   B They bought their new car ___three weeks ago___ .
   (three weeks)

2. **A** When did Lou and Angela get married?

   B They got married _____ .
   (four years)

3. **A** When did Angela have a baby?

   B She had a baby yesterday _____ .
   (8:20 a.m.)

4. **A** When did Lou begin his new job?

   B He began his new job _____ .
   (Tuesday)

5. **A** When did Lou move to the United States?

   B He moved to the United States _____ .
   (December 15th)

6. **A** When did Angela come to the United States?

   B She came to the United States _____ .
   (five years)

7. **A** When did Angela take the citizenship exam?

   B She took the citizenship exam _____ .
   (March)

Listen and repeat. Then practice with a partner.

CULTURE NOTE

The citizenship exam is a test you have to take to become an American citizen.

B Write. Complete the sentences. Use *at*, *in*, or *on*.

1. Anna graduated
   ___*in*___ 2003.

2. She got married
   _____ Saturday,
   August 16th,
   2006.

3. She had a baby
   _____ June
   21st, 2008,
   _____ 2:30 a.m.

4. She and her
   family moved
   to the United
   States _____
   2010.

5. She bought a
   house _____
   April.

6. She took the
   citizenship exam
   _____ May 16th.

7. She became a
   citizen _____
   Thursday.

8. She started
   her new job
   yesterday _____
   9:00 a.m.

Talk with a partner. Change the **bold** words and make conversations.
Use *before* or *after*.

> **A** When did Anna **graduate**?
> **B** She **graduated before** she
> moved to the United States.

1. graduate
2. buy a house
3. become a citizen

4. get married
5. take the citizenship exam
6. have a baby

3 Communicate

Read. What did you do? Check (✓) the boxes.

☐ get married
☐ have a baby
☐ get a driver's license
☐ get a new job

☐ register for English class
☐ buy a car
☐ move here
☐ study computers

> **USEFUL LANGUAGE**
>
> *I'm not married.*
> *I don't have any children.*
> *I didn't study computers.*

Talk with a partner. Ask and answer questions.

When did you get married?

I got married three years ago on August 25th.

☑ Use time phrases with *ago*, *on*, *in*, *at*, *before*, and *after*   **UNIT 6   75**

LESSON **D** Reading

1 Before you read

Look at the picture. Answer the questions.

1. Who are the people?
2. Where are they?
3. What are they doing?

2 Read

STUDENT TK 23
CLASS CD2 TK 5

Read the interview. Listen and read again.

An Interesting Life

Interviewer: What happened after you graduated from high school?

Olga: I went to university in Moscow, and I met my husband there. It was a long time ago! We were in the same class. We fell in love and got married on April 2nd, 1990. We had a small wedding in Moscow.

Interviewer: What happened after you got married?

Olga: I finished university and found a job. I was a teacher. Then, I had a baby. My husband and I were very excited to have a little boy.

Interviewer: When did you move to the United States?

Olga: We immigrated about 14 years ago. We became American citizens eight years ago.

> Skim: Read the questions. They tell you the focus of the interview.

3 After you read

A Write. Answer the questions about Olga. Write complete sentences.

1. When did Olga meet her husband? <u>*She met her husband a long time ago.*</u>
2. When did they get married? _____
3. When did they become American citizens? _____
4. When did she and her family move to the U.S.? _____

B Number the sentences in the correct order.

_____ Olga had a baby boy.   _____ She met her husband.

_____ She moved to the U.S.   _____ She became a U.S. citizen.

_____ She found a job.   <u>1</u> Olga graduated from high school.

_____ Olga got married.   _____ Olga finished university.

4 **Picture dictionary** Life events

1. _____retired_____

2. _____

3. _____

4. _____

5. _____

6. _____

7. _____

8. _____

9. _____

STUDENT TK 24
CLASS CD2 TK 6

A **Write** the words in the picture dictionary. Then listen and repeat.

fell in love	got married	immigrated
got divorced	got promoted	retired
got engaged	had a baby	started a business

B **Talk** with a partner. Which life events happened to you? When did they happen? What happened after that?

> I retired two years ago. After I retired, I started English classes.

☑ Read an interview about someone's life; use vocabulary for life events **UNIT 6** **77**

LESSON **E** Writing

1 Before you write

A **Talk** with a partner. Ask and answer the questions.

1. What three events were important in your life?
2. When was each event?

Write. Make a time line. Use your partner's information.

My partner's time line

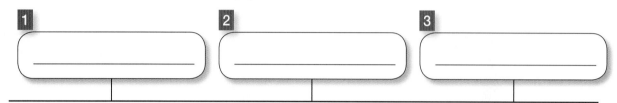

B **Read** about Bo-hai in his company newsletter.

COMPUTER SYSTEMS INC.

A New Employee: Bo-hai Cheng

I was born in 1990 in Beijing. I started university in 2008. I studied civil engineering. In 2011, I moved to Miami. After I moved, I bought a car. I also got engaged. Then I studied computers at a vocational school. I graduated on July 3rd. Three weeks ago, I found a computer job. In October, I'm going to get married!

C **Write.** Complete Bo-hai's time line.

| bought a car | graduated from vocational school | started university |
| found a job | moved to Miami | was born in 1990 |

Bo-hai's time line

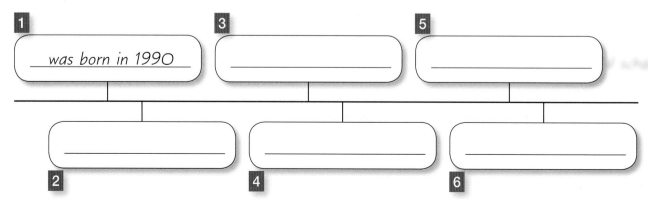

1 *was born in 1990*

D **Write** each sentence a different way.

1. I started college in 2008.
   In 2008, I started college.

2. In 2011, I moved to Miami.
   _____

3. I graduated on July 3rd.
   _____

4. Three weeks ago, I found a computer job.
   _____

5. In October, I'm going to get married.
   _____

> Use a comma (,) after time phrases like *In 2008* or *On July 3rd* at the beginning of a sentence.

E **Write.** Complete the time line about yourself.

My time line

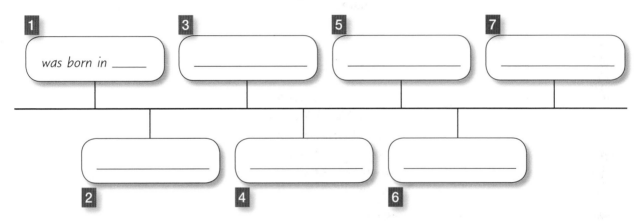

1. was born in _____
2. _____
3. _____
4. _____
5. _____
6. _____
7. _____

2 Write

Write a paragraph about yourself. Use Exercises 1B and 1E to help you.

3 After you write

A **Read** your paragraph to a partner.

B **Check** your partner's paragraph.

- What are the important events?
- What time phrases are in the paragraph?
- Are there commas after time phrases at the beginning of sentences?

LESSON F Another view

1 Life-skills reading

APPLICATION FOR A MARRIAGE LICENSE

Groom's Personal Data

1A. Name of Groom (First)	1B. Middle	1C. Last	2. Birthdate (Mo / Day / Yr)
Antonio	Marco	Velez	06/12/1988

3A. Residence (Street & Number)	3B. City	3C. Zip Code	3D. State	4. Place of Birth
406 E. 37th Street	Austin	78705	TX	Mexico City, Mexico

5. Number of Previous Marriages	6A. Last Marriage Ended by	6B. Date (Mo / Day / Yr)
1	Divorce	08/13/09

Bride's Personal Data

1A. Name of Bride (First)	1B. Middle	1C. Last	2. Birthdate (Mo / Day / Yr)
Maria	Luisa	Camacho	11/17/1992

3A. Residence (Street & Number)	3B. City	3C. Zip Code	3D. State	4. Place of Birth
1005 Hillside Oaks Drive	Austin	78710	TX	Lima, Peru

5. Number of Previous Marriages	6A. Last Marriage Ended by	6B. Date (Mo / Day / Yr)
None		

Groom's Driver's License / I.D.#:	Bride's Driver's License / I.D.#:
CO581316429	CO901516531

Ceremony Date:	Ceremony Location:
June 22, 2013	City Hall

A Read the questions. Look at the application for a marriage license. Fill in the answer.

1. When was the bride born?
   - Ⓐ in 1988
   - Ⓑ in 1992
   - Ⓒ in 1994
   - Ⓓ in 2007

2. When was the groom born?
   - Ⓐ on June 12, 1988
   - Ⓑ on December 6, 1988
   - Ⓒ on August 13, 2007
   - Ⓓ on November 17, 1992

3. When did the groom get divorced?
   - Ⓐ in 1997
   - Ⓑ in 2001
   - Ⓒ in 2009
   - Ⓓ in 2010

4. When is their wedding ceremony?
   - Ⓐ on 6/20/08
   - Ⓑ on 6/28/09
   - Ⓒ on 2/6/13
   - Ⓓ on 6/22/13

B Talk with a partner. Ask and answer the questions.

1. When was the last wedding you attended?
2. Where was the ceremony?
3. Who were the bride and groom? Where did they meet?

2 Grammar connections: *someone*, *some*, *anyone*, *everyone*, and *no one*

Use *someone*, *some*, *everyone*, and *no one* when you don't know who or don't say who.
Use *anyone* in the question.

Question	Answers	Class information
Is **anyone** from Haiti?	Yes, **someone** is from Haiti.	Lisette – Haiti Cesar – Mexico
	No, **no one** is from Haiti.	Cesar – Mexico Boris – Russia
	Yes, **everyone** is from Haiti.	Lisette – Haiti Ines – Haiti Franz– Haiti
	Yes, **some** are from Haiti.	Lisette – Haiti Ines – Haiti Cesar – Mexico

A **Work** in a group. Complete the chart.

A Are you married, Lisette?

B Yes, I am.

A Do you have children?

B No, I don't.

	(name)	(name)	(name)
1. Are you married?			
2. Are you single?			
3. Do you have children?			
4. Do you have a brother?			
5. Do you have a sister?			
6. Do you have grandchildren?			
7. Do you have a middle name?			

B **Share** your group's information with another group.

> In our group, everyone is married. No one is single . . .

3 Wrap up

Complete the **Self-assessment** on page 138.

Review

1 Listening

Read the questions. Then listen and circle the answers.

1. Where are Pablo and Marie?
   a. at a bus station
   (b.) at an airport

2. Why is Marie there?
   a. She just came back from Florida.
   b. She is meeting her parents.

3. How often does Marie visit her parents?
   a. every three months
   b. three times a year

4. Why is Pablo there?
   a. to meet Marie
   b. to meet his brother

5. How often does David visit?
   a. every weekend
   b. every vacation

6. How long does David usually stay?
   a. for three days
   b. for a week

Talk with a partner. Ask and answer the questions. Use complete sentences.

2 Grammar

A Write. Complete the story.

Christina's Last Vacation

Twice a year, Christina _____*takes*_____ a two-week vacation. Last year, she
                              1. take
_____ her brother in New York City. It _____ two days to get
    2. visit   3. take
there by train. She and her brother _____ a baseball game at Yankee
                                         4. see
Stadium and _____ to a concert in Central Park. It _____ a
                 5. go   6. be
great vacation. Christina always _____ a good time with her brother.
                                      7. have

B Write. Look at the answers. Write the questions.

1. **A** How often ____*does Christina take*____
   ___*a vacation*_____?
   B Christina takes a vacation twice a year.

2. **A** When _____
   B She visited her brother in New York
   City last year.

3. **A** How long _____?
   B It took two days to get there.

4. **A** Where _____?
   B They saw a baseball game at
   Yankee Stadium.

Talk with a partner. Ask and answer the questions.

3 Pronunciation: intonation in questions

CLASS CD2 TK 8

A **Listen** to the intonation in these questions.

> Where is the train station?

> Is the train station on Broadway or on Main Street?

CLASS CD2 TK 9

B **Listen and repeat.**

Wh- questions

   A How often do you eat at a restaurant?

   B Once a week.

Or questions

   A Do you eat at a restaurant once a week or once a month?

   B Once a week.

C **Talk** with a partner. Ask and answer the questions.

   1. How often do you take a vacation?

   2. Do you like to take a vacation in the summer or in the winter?

   3. When was your last vacation?

   4. Where did you go?

   5. Did you go alone or with your family?

   6. What did you do there?

D **Write** five questions. Make at least two questions using *or*.

1.
2.
3.
4.
5.

Talk with a partner. Ask and answer the questions.

> Do you take a bus or a train to school?

> I take a bus.

LESSON **A**
Listening

1 **Before you listen**

A Look at the picture. What do you see?

B Point to: a customer • a piano • appliances • a sofa
furniture • a price tag • a salesperson • a stove

C Describe the furniture. How much do the items cost?

USED FURNITURE
BIGGEST SALE OF THE YEAR!

$99

$230

$105

$22

$185

APPLIANCES

$700

$95

$1200
$960

PIANOS

$25

$69

$49.99

$1000

Nick

SALE!
20% OFF

$23

$400

Mike

WE HAVE THE
LOWEST PRICES!

Denise

Unit Goals
Identify furniture and other household items
Compare things
Interpret information on a sales receipt

UNIT 7

2 Listen

STUDENT TK 25
CLASS CD2 TK 10

A **Listen.** What are Nick and Denise talking about? Write the letter of the conversation.

1. _____

2. _____

3. _____

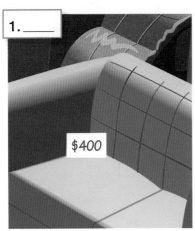

$400

~~$1200~~
$960

SALE!
20% OFF

STUDENT TK 25
CLASS CD2 TK 10

B **Listen again.** Write *T* (true) or *F* (false).

Conversation A

1. Denise and Nick need furniture.   _T_

2. Denise and Nick bought a house two days ago.   _____

3. Only the furniture is marked down 20 percent.   _____

Conversation B

4. Denise likes the brown sofa.   _____

5. Nick wants a big sofa.   _____

6. Denise likes the blue sofa.   _____

Conversation C

7. Denise and Nick need a piano.   _____

8. The upright piano is very old.   _____

9. The sound of the smaller piano is better.   _____

Listen again. Check your answers. Correct the false statements.

3 After you listen

Talk with a partner. Ask and answer the questions.

1. What are some good ways to find furniture?

2. Did you ever buy furniture in this country?

3. What did you buy?

> **CULTURE NOTE**
>
> Some stores in the U.S. sell furniture and appliances that are not new. They are called secondhand, thrift, or consignment stores. Their prices are cheaper.

LESSON **B** The blue sofa is smaller.

1 Grammar focus: comparatives

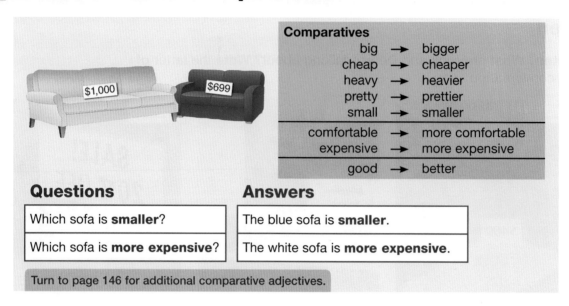

Comparatives

big	→	bigger
cheap	→	cheaper
heavy	→	heavier
pretty	→	prettier
small	→	smaller
comfortable	→	more comfortable
expensive	→	more expensive
good	→	better

Questions

Which sofa is **smaller**?
Which sofa is **more expensive**?

Answers

The blue sofa is **smaller**.
The white sofa is **more expensive**.

Turn to page 146 for additional comparative adjectives.

2 Practice

A Write. Complete the conversations. Use comparatives.

1. A Which sofa is more comfortable?

   B *The green striped sofa is more comfortable.*
   (green striped sofa / blue plaid sofa)

2. A Which chair is heavier?

   B _____
   (orange chair / purple chair)

3. A Which refrigerator is more expensive?

   B _____
   (small refrigerator / large refrigerator)

4. A Which table is bigger?

   B _____
   (square table / round table)

5. A Which stove is better?

   B _____
   (white stove / black stove)

6. A Which lamp is taller?

   B _____
   (floor lamp / table lamp)

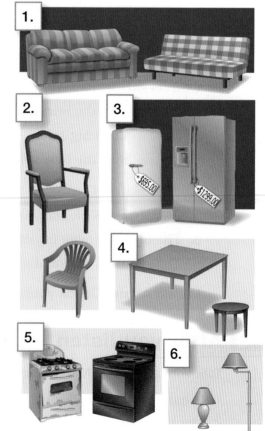

Listen and repeat. Then practice with a partner.

B **Talk** with a partner. Change the **bold** words and make conversations.

$299.00
dining table

$99.95
kitchen table

$75.99
desk lamp

$49.95
floor lamp

A Which **table** is **heavier**?
B The **dining table** is **heavier**.

1. table / heavy
2. table / small
3. table / expensive
4. table / long

5. lamp / short
6. lamp / pretty
7. lamp / cheap
8. lamp / good

USEFUL LANGUAGE

The dining table
is heavier.

The dining table is heavier
than the kitchen table.

3 Communicate

Talk with a partner. Compare the furniture in each store window.

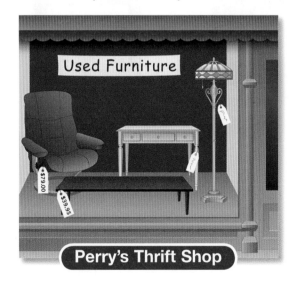
Perry's Thrift Shop

Greg's Used-Furniture Mart

A I like the **lamp** at **Perry's Thrift Shop**.
B Why?
A It's **prettier**.

☑ Use the comparative form of adjectives **UNIT 7** **87**

LESSON C The yellow chair is the cheapest.

1 Grammar focus: superlatives

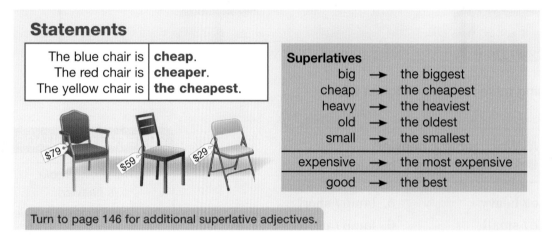

Statements

The blue chair is	cheap.
The red chair is	cheaper.
The yellow chair is	the cheapest.

$79 $59 $29

Superlatives

big	→	the biggest
cheap	→	the cheapest
heavy	→	the heaviest
old	→	the oldest
small	→	the smallest
expensive	→	the most expensive
good	→	the best

Turn to page 146 for additional superlative adjectives.

2 Practice

A Write. Complete the conversations. Use superlatives.

$1,995.00 $75.00 $199.99

1. **A** Which TV is ___the cheapest___?
   (cheap)

   B _The second TV is the cheapest._

2. **A** Which TV is _____?
   (heavy)

   B _____

3. **A** Which TV is _____?
   (expensive)

   B _____

4. **A** Which TV is _____?
   (old)

   B _____

5. **A** Which TV is _____?
   (small)

   B _____

6. **A** Which TV is _____?
   (big)

   B _____

CLASS CD2 TK 12

Listen and repeat. Then practice with a partner.

B **Write.** Complete the conversation. Use superlatives.

A This is ___the newest___ shopping mall in the city.
1. new
It's great.

USEFUL LANGUAGE

It has low prices.
It has cheap prices.

B Where's _____ place to buy clothes?
2. good

A Well, there are three clothing stores. Mega Store is _____ one.
3. big

It usually has _____ prices, but it's _____.
4. low   5. crowded

I never go there.

B What about Cleo's Boutique?

A Cleo's Boutique is _____ store. It's nice, but it's _____.
6. beautiful   7. expensive

B What about Madison's?

A Well, it's _____, but it's my favorite. It has
8. small

_____ clothes and _____ salespeople.
9. nice   10. friendly

B Look! Madison's is having a big sale. Let's go!

CLASS CD2 TK 13

Listen and check your answers. Then practice with a partner.

3 Communicate

Talk in a group. Ask and answer the questions about places in your community.

1. Which clothing store is the biggest?
2. Which clothing store has the lowest prices?
3. Which supermarket is the cheapest?
4. Which restaurant is the best?

☑ Use the superlative form of adjectives **UNIT 7** **89**

LESSON **D** Reading

1 Before you read

Look at the picture. Answer the questions.

1. Who is the woman?
2. What did she buy?

2 Read

STUDENT TK 26
CLASS CD2 TK 14

Read the newspaper article. Listen and read again.

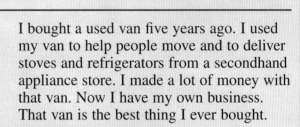

Today's Question
What's the best thing you ever bought?

The best thing I ever bought was an old piano. I bought it in a used-furniture store last month. It was the most beautiful piano in the store, but it wasn't very expensive. It has a beautiful sound. Now my two children are taking piano lessons. I love to hear music in the house.

Denise Robinson
Charleston, SC

I bought a used van five years ago. I used my van to help people move and to deliver stoves and refrigerators from a secondhand appliance store. I made a lot of money with that van. Now I have my own business. That van is the best thing I ever bought.

Sammy Chin
Myrtle Beach, SC

> Guess the meaning of new words from other words nearby.
> *appliances = stoves, refrigerators*

3 After you read

Write. Answer the questions about the article. Write complete sentences.

1. What did Denise buy? *She bought an old piano.* _____
2. What did Sammy buy? _____
3. Who is taking piano lessons? _____
4. Who has a business? _____
5. Which was probably more expensive – the piano or the van? _____

_____

4 Picture dictionary Furniture

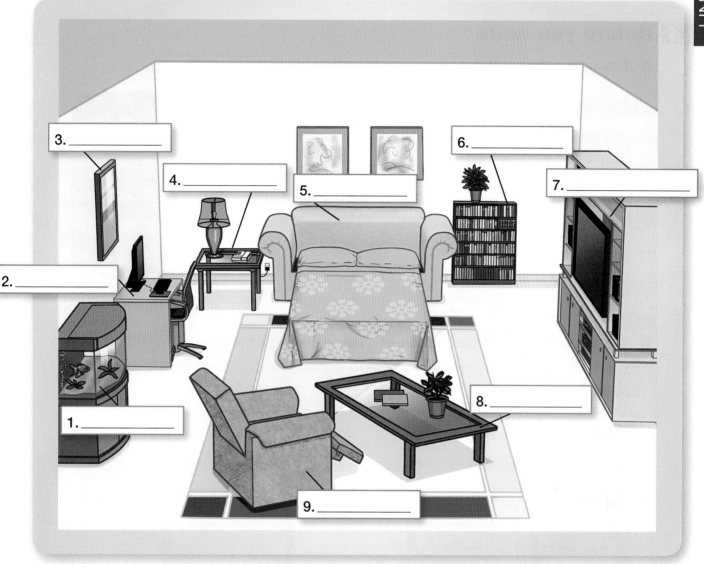

3. _____

4. _____

5. _____

6. _____

7. _____

2. _____

8. _____

1. _____

9. _____

STUDENT TK 27
CLASS CD2 TK 15

A Write the words in the picture dictionary. Then listen and repeat.

aquarium	computer desk	mirror
bookcase	end table	recliner
coffee table	entertainment center	sofa bed

B Talk with a partner. Change the **bold** words and make conversations.

> A Which is **bigger**, the **coffee table** or the **end table**?
> B The **coffee table** is **bigger**.

> A Do you like the **bookcase**?
> B **Yes, I do.** It's **nicer** than my **bookcase**.

☑ Read an article about purchases; use vocabulary for furniture   **UNIT 7   91**

LESSON **E** Writing

1 Before you write

A Talk with a partner. These items are gifts. Which gift is the best? Tell why.

1.

2.

3.

B Talk with three classmates. Ask questions and complete the chart.

1. What's the best gift you ever received?
2. Who gave it to you?
3. When did you receive this gift?
4. Why was it the best gift?

Name	Paolo			
Best gift	a trip to Brazil			
From	his wife			
When	last summer			
Why	because he saw his parents again			

Talk. Share your information with the class.

> Paolo's best gift was a trip to Brazil last summer. His wife gave it to him. It was the best gift because he saw his parents again.

C **Read** the story. Complete the sentences.

ago	heart	necklace
birthday	mother	store

The Best Gift

The best gift I ever received was a ___*necklace*___.

1

My _____ bought it in a jewelry _____.

2 3

The necklace was in the shape of a _____.

4

She gave it to me for my _____ a long

5

time _____. My mother said it was her heart. It was the

6

best gift because it was from her.

D **Write.** Answer the questions about yourself.

1. What is the best gift you ever received? _____
2. Who gave it to you? _____
3. Where did the gift come from? _____
4. When did you receive this gift? _____
5. Why was it the best gift? _____

2 Write

Write a paragraph about the best gift you ever received.
Use Exercises 1C and 1D to help you.

> Use *because* to answer the question *Why* and to give a reason.
>
> *It was the best gift because it was beautiful.*

3 After you write

A **Read** your paragraph to a partner.

B **Check** your partner's paragraph.

- What was the gift?
- Why was it the best gift?
- Did your partner use *because* to say why?

LESSON F Another view

Life-skills reading

SALES RECEIPT

Al's Discount Furniture
2100 Willow Boulevard
Charleston, SC 29401
(843) 555-0936

Sold to:
Nick Robinson
2718 Central Avenue
Charleston, SC 29412

Item #	Description	Price
1.	Green sofa	$699.00
2.	Coffee table	$295.00
3.	Table lamp	$39.95
4.	Bookcase	$149.00
	Subtotal Sales tax 8.5%	$1,182.95 $100.55
	TOTAL	**$1,283.50**
	VISTA/MASTER CHARGE	$1,283.50

No refunds or exchanges after 30 days.

A Read the questions. Look at the sales receipt. Fill in the answer.

1. Which is the cheapest item?
   - Ⓐ the green sofa
   - Ⓑ the bookcase
   - Ⓒ the coffee table
   - Ⓓ the table lamp

2. Which is the most expensive item?
   - Ⓐ the green sofa
   - Ⓑ the bookcase
   - Ⓒ the coffee table
   - Ⓓ the table lamp

3. When can a customer *not* exchange an item?
   - Ⓐ after 7 days
   - Ⓑ after 15 days
   - Ⓒ after 30 days
   - Ⓓ before 30 days

4. What is the total of the receipt?
   - Ⓐ $100.55
   - Ⓑ $699.00
   - Ⓒ $1,182.95
   - Ⓓ $1,283.50

B Talk with a partner. Ask and answer the questions.

1. What percent is the sales tax on the receipt for Al's Discount Furniture?
2. What percent is the sales tax in your town or city?
3. Did you buy any furniture this year? What did you buy?

2 Grammar connections: *one*, *the other*, *some*, *the others*

The pronouns *one*, *the other*, *some*, and *the others* can replace nouns.

There are two shoe stores.

{ One shoe store / **One** } has men's shoes, and { the other shoe store / **the other** } has women's shoes.

There are many restaurants.

{ Some restaurants / **Some** } have fast food, and { the other restaurants / **the others** } have international food.

A Work with a partner. Look at the stores in a mall directory. Talk about what they have. Take turns.

A There are two shoe stores.

B Yes. *One* has men's shoes, and *the other* has women's shoes.
There are five restaurants in the food court.

A Yes. *Some* have fast food, and *the others* have international food.

Directory of Stores

SHOE STORES
Men's
The Shoe Place

Women's
Shoe Time

CLOTHING STORES
Women's
Victoria Dresses
California Style

Men's
Jack's Jeans
The Modern Man

HOUSEWARE STORES
Kitchen
Ned's Kitchen

Bed and Bath
Home Touch

ELECTRONICS STORES
Computers
Computer Center
T-Plus

Wireless
Horizon Phones
Mega Metro Phones

FURNITURE STORES
Beautiful Bedrooms
Sofa World

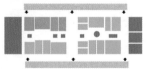

FOOD COURT
Fast Food
Chicken-To-Go
Fast and Now
Sandwich Plus

International Food
Food Palace
Pasta House

B Work with your partner. Look at the picture. Make sentences with *one*, *the other*, *some*, and *the others*.

A There are two dresses. One is red, and the other is black.

B Yes, and one is long, and the other is short.

3 Wrap up

Complete the **Self-assessment** on page 139.

LESSON **A**
Listening

1 **Before you listen**

A Look at the picture. What do you see?

B Point to: a lab • linens • a patient • a walker supplies • co-workers • an orderly • a wheelchair

C Look at these people. What are they doing?

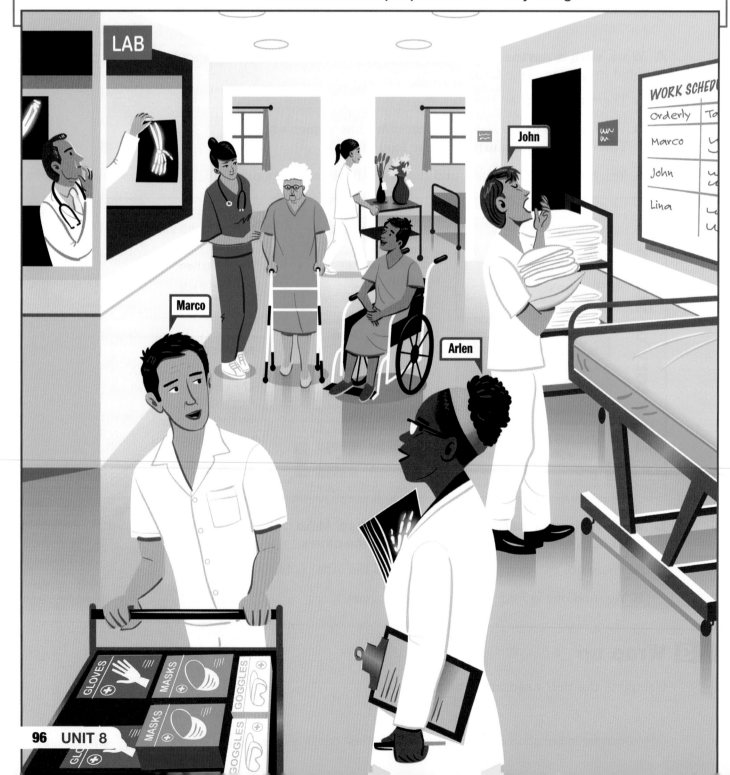

Unit Goals

Describe job duties
Describe past activities
Interpret information on a weekly time sheet

UNIT 8

2 Listen

A Listen. What is Marco talking about? Write the letter of the conversation.

STUDENT TK 28
CLASS CD2 TK 16

1. _____

2. _____

3. _____

B Listen again. Write *T* (true) or *F* (false).

STUDENT TK 28
CLASS CD2 TK 16

Conversation A

1. Marco picked up X-rays this morning.   *T*
2. Marco delivered linens to the third floor.   ____
3. Marco needs to prepare rooms on the second floor.   ____

Conversation B

4. John is tired.   ____
5. Marco worked the night shift.   ____
6. Marco wants to go back to school.   ____

> **CULTURE** NOTE
>
> People who work at night work the *night shift*.

Conversation C

7. Suzanne works in Human Resources.   ____
8. Marco wants to be a nurse.   ____
9. Marco wants to work full-time.   ____

Listen again. Check your answers. Correct the false statements.

3 After you listen

Talk with a partner. Ask and answer the questions.

1. Do you have a job? What do you do?
2. Did you have a job before? What did you do?
3. What job do you want in the future?

LESSON **B** Where did you go last night?

1 Grammar focus: *What* and *Where* questions and simple past

Questions		
What did	you	**do** yesterday?
	he	
	they	

Answers	
I	**worked**.
He	
They	

Regular verbs
clean → cleaned
deliver → delivered
help → helped
pick up → picked up
prepare → prepared

Questions		
Where did	you	**go** last night?
	she	
	they	

Answers	
I	**went** to a meeting.
She	
They	

Irregular verbs
go → went
make → made
meet → met
take → took

Turn to page 143 for complete grammar charts.

2 Practice

A **Write.** Complete the conversations. Use *What* or *Where* and the simple past.

1. **A** ___*What*___ did Linda do after breakfast?

    B She ___*made*___ the beds.
    (make)

2. **A** _____ did Brenda and Leo do this morning?

    B They _____ patients in the reception area.
    (pick up)

3. **A** _____ did Trevor do this morning?

    B He _____ X-rays.
    (deliver)

4. **A** _____ did Jill and Brad take the linens?

    B They _____ the linens to the second floor.
    (take)

5. **A** _____ did Felix do yesterday?

    B He _____ patients with their walkers and wheelchairs.
    (help)

6. **A** _____ did Juan and Ivana go after work?

    B They _____ to the coffee shop across the street.
    (go)

 Listen and repeat. Then practice with a partner.

3 Pronunciation: the *-ed* ending in regular simple past verbs

A **Listen** to the *-ed* endings in these simple past verbs.

CLASS CD2 TK 22

/d/	/t/	/ɪd/
us**ed**	help**ed**	want**ed**
She used the new machine.	He helped the nurses.	They wanted to make the beds.
deliver**ed**	work**ed**	assist**ed**
You delivered the mail.	He worked on the weekends.	She assisted the patient.

B **Listen and repeat.**

CLASS CD2 TK 23

/d/	/t/	/ɪd/
repaired	picked	needed
prepared	cooked	started
played	walked	visited

C **Listen** and check (✓) the correct column.

CLASS CD2 TK 24

	/d/	/t/	/ɪd/		/d/	/t/	/ɪd/
1. cleaned	✓			5. pushed			
2. operated				6. checked			
3. finished				7. answered			
4. handled				8. reported			

D **Write** six regular verbs from Units 7 and 8 in the simple past. Check (✓) the correct column.

	/d/	/t/	/ɪd/		/d/	/t/	/ɪd/
1.				4.			
2.				5.			
3.				6.			

Talk with a partner. Make a sentence with each verb. Take turns.

LESSON **A**
Listening

1 **Before you listen**

A Look at the picture. What do you see?

B Point to: a dishwasher • a leak • a lightbulb • a lock • a dryer
garbage • a sink • a washing machine

C Look at the woman. What's she doing?

2 Listen

STUDENT TK 31
CLASS CD2 TK 25

A Listen. Who is Stella talking to? Write the letter of the conversation.

1. ____

2. ____  MANAGEMENT

Rentals

| Houses | Apartments |

3. ____  BROWN'S PLUMBING SERVICE

STUDENT TK 31
CLASS CD2 TK 25

B Listen again. Write *T* (true) or *F* (false).

Conversation A

1. Stella lives in Apartment 4B.   *T*

2. Stella is talking to a plumber.   ____

3. Don Brown is a neighbor.   ____

Conversation B

4. Stella wants to speak to her husband.   ____

5. Don Brown will come in one hour.   ____

6. Stella will unlock the door for the plumber. ____

Conversation C

7. Russell wants Stella to call a neighbor. ____

8. Stella already called the plumber.   ____

9. Stella is going to school.   ____

Listen again. Check your answers. Correct the false statements.

3 After you listen

Talk with a partner. Ask and answer the questions.

1. Who fixes things in your home?

2. Did you ever need to call a plumber or other repair person?

3. Who did you call?

4. What happened?

LESSON **B** Can you call a plumber, please?

1 Grammar focus: requests with *Can, Could, Will, Would*

Questions			Answers
Can			Sure. I'd be happy to.
Could	you	**call** a plumber, please?	Yes, of course.
Will			No, not now. Maybe later.
Would			Sorry, I can't right now.

2 Practice

A **Write.** Complete the conversations. Make requests with *can*, *could*, *will*, or *would*.

1. fix the dryer   2. unclog the sink   3. clean the carpet

4. fix the lock   5. fix the window   6. repair the dishwasher

1. **A** Could _you fix the dryer, please_?
   B Yes, of course.
2. **A** Can _____?
   B No, not now. Maybe later.
3. **A** Would _____?
   B Sorry, I can't right now.

4. **A** Will _____?
   B Sure. I'd be happy to.
5. **A** Could _____?
   B Yes, of course.
6. **A** Would _____?
   B Sure. I'd be happy to.

Listen and repeat. Then practice with a partner.

CLASS CD2 TK 26

B **Talk** with a partner. Change the **bold** words and make conversations.

A Can you **fix the window**, please?
B Yes, of course.

A Would you **fix the stove**, please?
B Sorry, I can't right now.

1. fix the window
2. repair the refrigerator
3. unclog the sink
4. fix the toilet

5. fix the stove
6. fix the light
7. call an electrician
8. repair the lock

3 Communicate

Write. What are some problems in your home or in a friend's home?
Make a list of requests for the landlord.

> Requests for the landlord
> 1. fix the window

CULTURE NOTE

A *tenant* rents an apartment or house from the *landlord*. The landlord is the owner.

Talk. Role-play with a partner. One person is the tenant. The other is the landlord.

Tenant: Could you fix the window, please?
Landlord: Yes, of course. I'll be there tomorrow.

LESSON **C** Which one do you recommend?

1 Grammar focus: *Which* questions and simple present

Questions

Which	plumbing service	**do**	you	recommend?
		does	he	
		do	they	

Answers

I	**recommend**	Purdy's Plumbing.
He	**recommends**	
They	**recommend**	

Turn to page 142 for a complete grammar chart.

2 Practice

CULTURE NOTE

Plumbers and electricians are usually licensed. You can ask to see their license.

HARRISON'S
Plumbing Service
555-8000   Clean and Professional

• $100 an hour
• Open 24 hours a day / 7 days a week
• Fast
• 30 years of experience

BROWN'S
Plumbing Service

• Complete plumbing service
• $50 an hour
• Licensed
• 15 years of experience
• Insured   555-7407

A Write. Complete the conversations. Use *Which* and the simple present.

1. A (you / recommend)
   Which plumbing service do you recommend — Harrison's or Brown's?

   B (cheaper) *I recommend Brown's Plumbing Service because it's cheaper.*

2. A (he / recommend) _____

   B (fast) _____

3. A (they / recommend) _____

   B (licensed) _____

4. A (she / recommend) _____

   B (insured) _____

5. A (they / recommend) _____

   B (experienced) _____

6. A (he / recommend) _____

   B (open 24 hours a day) _____

Listen and repeat. Then practice with a partner.

CLASS CD2 TK 27

B **Talk** with a partner. Change the **bold** words and make conversations.

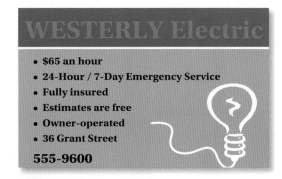

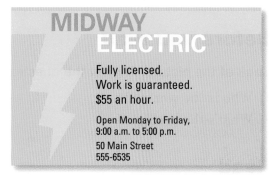

A Which electric service do you recommend?
B I recommend **Westerly Electric** because it's **open 24 hours a day**.

CULTURE NOTE

An *owner-operated* business is usually small and friendly.

1. open 24 hours a day
2. fully licensed
3. owner-operated
4. on Main Street
5. fully insured
6. cheaper

3 Communicate

For each place, write two or three names of businesses in your community.

1. supermarkets _____
2. restaurants _____
3. pharmacies _____
4. gas stations _____
5. banks _____
6. department stores _____
7. fast food restaurants _____
8. coffee shops _____

Talk with your classmates. Ask and answer questions about the places in your community.

Which supermarket do you like?

I like Acme Supermarket because it's cheap.

I prefer SaveMore Supermarket on Broadway because it's clean.

USEFUL LANGUAGE

I recommend . . .
I suggest . . .
I like . . .
I prefer . . .

LESSON **D** Reading

1 Before you read

Look at the picture. Answer the questions.

1. Who is the woman?
2. What's the problem?

2 Read

Read Stella's notice. Listen and read again.

STUDENT TK 32
CLASS CD2 TK 28

Attention, tenants:

**Do you have problems in your apartment?
Is anyone fixing them?**

- Many tenants have broken windows.
- Tenants on the third floor have no lights in the hall.
- A tenant on the second floor has a leaking ceiling.
- Tenants on the first floor smell garbage every day.

I'm really upset! We need to get together and write a
letter of complaint to the manager of the building.

Come to a meeting Friday night at 7:00 p.m. in
Apartment 4B.

Stella Taylor, Tenant 4B

> Sometimes it is not
> necessary to know
> the exact meaning of
> a word. It is enough to
> know if the meaning
> is positive (good) or
> negative (not good).
>
> *upset, complaint* =
> negative

3 After you read

Write. Answer the questions about Stella's notice. Write
complete sentences.

1. Which tenant has a leaking ceiling? *A tenant on the second floor has a leaking ceiling.*

2. Which tenants have no lights in the hall? _____

3. Which tenants smell garbage? _____

4. What does Stella want to write? _____

5. Where is the meeting? _____

4 Picture dictionary Home problems

1. _____ *broken* _____

2. _____

3. _____

4. _____

5. _____

6. _____

7. _____

8. _____

9. _____

STUDENT TK 33
CLASS CD2 TK 29

A **Write** the words in the picture dictionary. Then listen and repeat.

bent	cracked	scratched
broken	dripping	stained
burned out	jammed	torn

B **Talk** with a partner. Change the **bold** words and make conversations.

A What's the problem?
B **My window is broken.** Could you fix it, please?
A Sure. I'll try.

LESSON E Writing

1 Before you write

A **Talk** in a group. Ask and answer the questions.

1. Did you ever have a problem in your apartment?
2. What was the problem?
3. Did you tell the landlord about the problem?
4. Did you write a letter to the landlord?

B **Read** the letter of complaint.

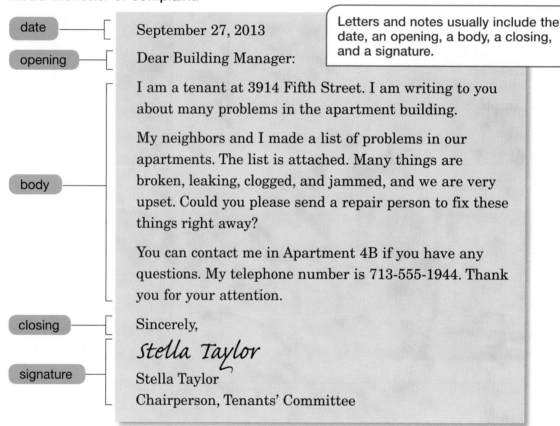

date — September 27, 2013

opening — Dear Building Manager:

Letters and notes usually include the date, an opening, a body, a closing, and a signature.

body —

I am a tenant at 3914 Fifth Street. I am writing to you about many problems in the apartment building.

My neighbors and I made a list of problems in our apartments. The list is attached. Many things are broken, leaking, clogged, and jammed, and we are very upset. Could you please send a repair person to fix these things right away?

You can contact me in Apartment 4B if you have any questions. My telephone number is 713-555-1944. Thank you for your attention.

closing — Sincerely,

signature —

Stella Taylor

Stella Taylor
Chairperson, Tenants' Committee

C **Write.** Answer the questions about Stella's letter.

1. What is the date of this letter? *September 27, 2013.* _____
2. Who is the letter to? _____
3. Who is the letter from? _____
4. How many paragraphs are in the body of the letter? _____
5. What is the closing? _____

D **Write.** Read the list of problems. Complete the sentences.

| broken | clogged | cracked | jammed | leaking | stained |

Problems at 3914 Fifth Street

Apartment 1F

The carpet is ———————————.
1

Apartment 2C

The front door lock is ———————.
2

Apartment 3A

The bedroom walls are ——————.
3

Apartment 4B

The living room window is —————.
4

Apartment 5B

The refrigerator is ———————.
5

Apartment 6D

The kitchen sink is ———————.
6

1.

2.

3.

4.

5.

6.

2 Write

Write a letter of complaint to your building manager or landlord. Use Exercises 1B and 1D to help you.

3 After you write

A **Read** your letter to a partner.

B **Check** your partner's letter.

- What are the problems?
- Who is the letter to?
- Does the letter have an opening and a closing?

LESSON F Another view

A+ PLUMBING REPAIRS	Customer Invoice 102051

A+ PLUMBING REPAIRS
Montague, New Jersey 07827

Free Estimates
We charge less and don't leave a mess!
(973) 555-2399 • 30-day guarantee on all repairs

Customer Name *Victor Waters*

Customer Address *1872 Valley Street*
Newton, New Jersey 07860

Service Technician *Russ*

Description of Problem		Actual Cost
Sink Clogged		$35.00
Bathroom Shower Leaking		$50.00
Dishwasher Overflowed		$60.00
	Total	$145.00

A **Read** the questions. Look at the invoice. Fill in the answer.

1. How much is the total?
   - Ⓐ $35.00
   - Ⓑ $50.00
   - Ⓒ $60.00
   - Ⓓ $145.00

2. How much did it cost to fix the dishwasher?
   - Ⓐ $35.00
   - Ⓑ $50.00
   - Ⓒ $60.00
   - Ⓓ $145.00

3. What was leaking?
   - Ⓐ the bathroom shower
   - Ⓑ the dishwasher
   - Ⓒ the sink
   - Ⓓ the washing machine

4. Which repair was the most expensive?
   - Ⓐ the dishwasher
   - Ⓑ the bathroom shower
   - Ⓒ the dryer
   - Ⓓ the sink

B **Talk** with a partner. Ask and answer the questions.

1. What repair problems do you sometimes have?
2. Can you repair things in your home?
3. Do you have a friend or family member who can repair things?
4. What does that person help you with?

2 Grammar connections: *let's* and *let's not*

Use *let's* + verb and *let's not* + verb to make suggestions.
Let's buy a new refrigerator.
Let's not fix the dishwasher.

A Work in a group. Look at the kitchen and the list. You have $2,000. What do you want to buy, change, or fix? Make suggestions.

A *Let's buy* a new refrigerator.

B Great. *Let's do* that.

C No, *let's not get* a new one. It's too expensive. *Let's repair* the old one.

2 cans of paint	$65
New table	$150
New chairs	$50 each
New refrigerator	$950
Refrigerator repair	$300
New stove	$599
Stove repair	$200
New dishwasher	$549
Dishwasher repair	$200
New sink	$400
Sink repair	$150
New window	$350
Light	$45 each
Lightbulb	$5 each

B Work in your group. Think of ways to improve your classroom.

A Let's bring more books in English for people to read.

B Let's get some free magazines.

3 Wrap up

Complete the **Self-assessment** on page 140.

LESSON A
Listening

1 Before you listen

A Look at the picture. What do you see?

B Point to: a card • a graduation cake • flowers • a guest
perfume • a piece of cake • balloons • a present

C Look at the people. What are they doing?

Unit Goals
Discuss celebrations such as graduation
Write a thank-you note
Interpret information on a party invitation

UNIT 10

2 Listen

STUDENT TK 34
CLASS CD2 TK 30

A Listen. Which gift is Celia talking about? Write the letter of the conversation.

1. ____

2. ____

3. ____

STUDENT TK 34
CLASS CD2 TK 30

B Listen again. Write *T* (true) or *F* (false).

Conversation A

1. Celia is having a birthday party.   *F*

2. Celia's mother made a cake.   ____

3. Aunt Ana would like some cake.   ____

Conversation B

4. Mrs. Campbell is a student.   ____

5. Celia started English class three years ago.   ____

6. Mrs. Campbell brought Celia a card.   ____

Conversation C

7. Sue brought her children to the party.   ____

8. Sue would like some water.   ____

9. Sue gave Celia some balloons.   ____

Listen again. Check your answers. Correct the false statements.

3 After you listen

Talk with a partner. Ask and answer the questions.

1. Does your family celebrate graduations?

2. How does your family celebrate them?

3. What other special days does your family celebrate?

CULTURE NOTE

People often celebrate someone's graduation with a party for family and friends.

☑ Listen for and identify information about people at a party   **UNIT 10   123**

LESSON **B** Would you like some cake?

1 Grammar focus: *Would you like . . . ?*

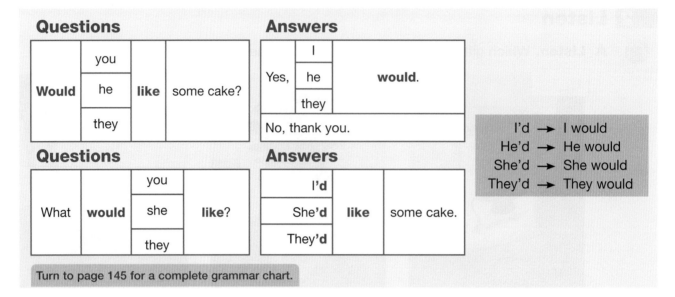

Questions

Would	you	like	some cake?
	he		
	they		

Answers

Yes,	I	would.
	he	
	they	

| No, thank you. | | |

Questions

What	would	you	like?
		she	
		they	

Answers

I'd	like	some cake.
She'd		
They'd		

I'd → I would
He'd → He would
She'd → She would
They'd → They would

Turn to page 145 for a complete grammar chart.

2 Practice

A Write. Complete the conversations.

1. **A** ___Would you like___ a cup of coffee?
   (you)

   B Yes, ___I would___.

2. **A** _____ a balloon?
   (he)

   B Yes, _____.

3. **A** _____ some ice cream?
   (she)

   B Yes, _____.

4. **A** _____ a sandwich?
   (you)

   B No, _____. I'm full.

5. **A** _____ some salad?
   (they)

   B Yes, _____.

6. **A** _____ a hot dog?
   (he)

   B No, _____. He just ate one.

Listen and repeat. Then practice with a partner.

CLASS CD2 TK 31

B **Talk** with a partner. Change the **bold** words and make conversations.

A What would **you** like?
B **I'd** like **some cake**, please.

1. you / some cake

2. they / some fruit

3. she / a piece of pie

4. they / some cheese

5. he / a bottle of water

6. you / some cookies

7. he / some soda

8. she / some dessert

9. you / a cup of tea

3 | Communicate

Talk with a partner. Make conversations.

A Would you like something to drink?
B Yes, please.
A What would you like?
B I'd like some soda, please.
A Would you like something to eat?
B No, thank you. I'm full.

USEFUL LANGUAGE

Would you like something to drink?

Would you like something to eat?

Yes, please. / No, thank you. I'm full.

☑ Use *would you like* to make offers   **UNIT 10**   **125**

LESSON **C** Tim gave Mary a present.

1 Grammar focus: direct and indirect objects

Statements

| Tim | gave
bought | a present | to
for | **Mary**.
her. |

| Tim | gave
bought | **Mary**
her | a present. |

Turn to page 145 for a complete grammar chart.

Irregular verbs
buy → bought
give → gave
send → sent
write → wrote

give + to = give **to** someone
buy + for = buy **for** someone

2 Practice

A **Write.** Look at Joe's "to do" list. What did he do yesterday? Write sentences.

To do

✓ *buy flowers for Sylvia*

✓ *buy a card for Nick*

✓ *write a letter to Pam*

✓ *buy a cake for Mary and Judy*

✓ *give roses to Eva*

✓ *send an invitation to Paul*

1. *Joe bought flowers for Sylvia.*
2. _____
3. _____
4. _____
5. _____
6. _____

Write. Complete the conversations.

1. **A** What did Joe buy Sylvia?
   B *Joe bought Sylvia flowers.*

2. **A** What did Joe buy Nick?
   B _____

3. **A** What did Joe write Pam?
   B _____

4. **A** What did Joe buy Mary and Judy?
   B _____

5. **A** What did Joe give Eva?
   B _____

6. **A** What did Joe send Paul?
   B _____

Listen and repeat. Then practice with a partner.

CLASS CD2 TK 32

B **Talk** with a partner. Change the **bold** words and make conversations.

1. some balloons

2. a card

3. some flowers

4. some cookies

5. some perfume

6. some books

A What did you give **Daniel**?
B I gave **him some balloons**.
A That's nice.

USEFUL LANGUAGE

I	→	me
he	→	him
she	→	her
they	→	them

3 Communicate

Write. Choose three classmates. Choose three items from your desk. Give one thing to each classmate. Then complete the chart.

Classmates	Items
Anika	my Ventures book
1.	
2.	
3.	

Talk with a partner. Share your information.

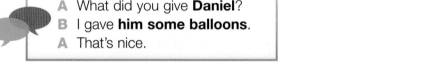

I gave Anika my *Ventures* book.

I gave Rudy my pen.

Ask for your things back.

Anika, please give me my *Ventures* book.

Rudy, please give me my pen.

LESSON **D** Reading

1 Before you read

Look at the picture. Answer the questions.

1. Who is the woman?

2. What is she doing?

2 Read

Read the paragraph. Listen and read again.

STUDENT TK 35
CLASS CD2 TK 33

Look for examples of the main idea when you read. This paragraph is about gifts.
Look for examples of all the gifts.

Graduation Party Gifts

I had a graduation party last Friday. My husband sent invitations to my teacher and to my relatives and friends. They all came to the party! Some guests brought gifts for me. My teacher Mrs. Campbell gave me a card. My Aunt Ana brought me flowers. My friend Sue gave me some perfume. My classmate Ruth brought me some cookies. After the party, I wrote them thank-you notes. Tomorrow, I'm going to mail the thank-you notes at the post office.

3 After you read

Write. Answer the questions about Celia's graduation party.
Write complete sentences.

1. When was Celia's graduation party? _Celia's graduation party was last Friday._

2. Who came to the party? _____

3. What did Mrs. Campbell give Celia? _____

4. What did Sue give Celia? _____

5. What did Ruth give Celia? _____

6. What is Celia going to do tomorrow? _____

4 **Picture dictionary** Celebrations

1. _____Thanksgiving_____

2. _____

3. _____

4. _____

5. _____

6. _____

7. _____

8. _____

9. _____

STUDENT TK 36
CLASS CD2 TK 34

A **Write** the words in the picture dictionary. Then listen and repeat.

a baby shower	Independence Day	Thanksgiving
Halloween	Mother's Day	Valentine's Day
a housewarming	New Year's Eve	a wedding

B **Talk** with a partner. What special days do you celebrate? How do you celebrate them?

> Do you celebrate Thanksgiving?

> Yes, we do. We always go to my mother-in-law's house for a big turkey dinner.

☑ Read a narrative paragraph about a party; use vocabulary for celebrations **UNIT 10** **129**

LESSON **E** Writing

1 Before you write

A **Talk** with a partner. Ask and answer the questions.

1. Did you ever receive a thank-you note?
2. Did you ever send someone a thank-you note?
3. In other countries, when do people write thank-you notes?

B **Read** the thank-you note.

> Indent the paragraphs in an informal note. Place the date on the right side. Don't indent *Dear____*.

June 30, 2013

Dear Aunt Ana,

Thank you for the lovely flowers you gave me for my graduation. They are beautiful! I really like the color of the roses. Red is my favorite color!

Thank you so much for coming to my graduation party. I hope you had a good time.

Love,
Celia

> **CULTURE NOTE**
>
> People often write thank-you notes. A thank-you note identifies the gift and says something about why you like it. It is polite to thank someone for a gift.

C **Write.** Answer the questions about Celia's note. Write complete sentences.

1. When did Celia write the note?

   Celia wrote the note on June 30, 2013.

2. Who did Celia write the note to?

   _____

3. What did Aunt Ana give Celia?

   _____

4. Why did Celia like the gift?

   _____

D Write. Complete the thank-you note.

Best wishes	color	fun	shirt
birthday	Dear	party	size

_____ (today's date)

_____ John,
      1

    Thank you for the beautiful _____ you gave me for
                                  2

my _____. It is just the right _____.
    3   4

I also really like the _____.
                        5

    Thank you so much for coming to my _____.
                                      6

I hope you had _____.
               7

_____,
        8
    Paula

> **CULTURE NOTE**
>
> Use *Love* or *Best wishes* in a personal note. Use *Sincerely* in a formal letter.

E Write. Answer the questions.

1. When did a friend give you a present? _____

2. What is your friend's name? _____

3. What was the present? _____

4. Why did you like the present? _____

5. What was the celebration? _____

2 Write

Write a thank-you note to a friend for a gift. Use Exercises 1B, 1D, and 1E to help you.

3 After you write

A Read your note to a partner.

B Check your partner's note.

- What was the present?
- What was the celebration?
- Did your partner indent each paragraph?

LESSON F Another view

1 Life-skills reading

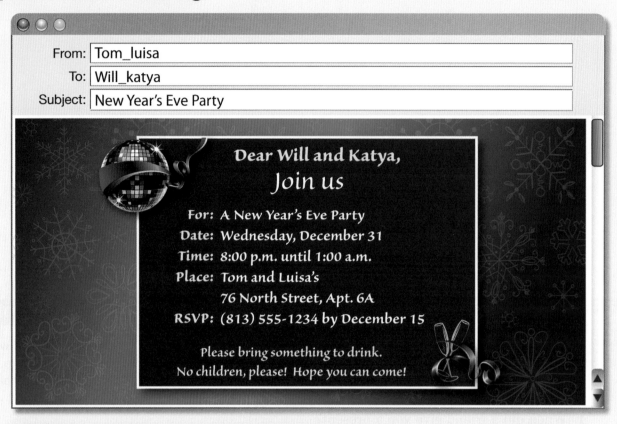

From: Tom_luisa

To: Will_katya

Subject: New Year's Eve Party

Dear Will and Katya,

Join us

For: A New Year's Eve Party
Date: Wednesday, December 31
Time: 8:00 p.m. until 1:00 a.m.
Place: Tom and Luisa's
76 North Street, Apt. 6A
RSVP: (813) 555-1234 by December 15

Please bring something to drink.
No children, please! Hope you can come!

A Read the questions. Look at the invitation. Fill in the answer.

1. Who is giving the party?

   (A) Luisa

   (B) Tom and Luisa

   (C) Will and Katya

   (D) Will and Luisa

2. When do people need to say *yes* or *no* to the invitation?

   (A) before December 15

   (B) after December 15

   (C) on December 31

   (D) after December 31

3. What time will the party begin?

   (A) 8:00 a.m.

   (B) 1:00 p.m.

   (C) 8:00 p.m.

   (D) 1:00 a.m.

4. What should people bring to the party?

   (A) something to drink

   (B) something to eat

   (C) their children

   (D) nothing

B Talk in a group. Ask and answer the questions.

1. Do you like to go to parties? Do you like to give parties?

2. Do you usually bring something to a party? What do you bring?

3. Tell about the last party you went to.

2 Grammar connections: *there is / there are* and *there was / there were*

Present	Past
There is a small cake on the table. **There isn't** any ice cream on the table.	**There was** a big cake on the table. **There wasn't** any fruit on the table.
There are four people at the party. **There aren't** any presents on the table.	**There were** six children at the party. **There weren't** any cards on the table.

A Work with a partner. Look at the pictures. Identify the differences. How many are there?

Today

1980

B Work with your partner. Talk about each difference. Take turns.

A The cakes are different. There's a small cake on the table today.

B There wasn't a small cake in 1980. There was a big birthday cake.

3 Wrap up

Complete the **Self-assessment** on page 140.

Review

1 Listening

Read the questions. Then listen and circle the answers.

1. Why is Ramona going to have a party?
   a. to celebrate her birthday
   (b.) to celebrate her new apartment

2. When is Ramona's party?
   a. next month
   b. next week

3. What does Ramona want to do?
   a. get her apartment ready
   b. fix the windows

4. How many good painters does Fabio know?
   a. one
   b. two

5. What is the name of the first painter?
   a. Fabio
   b. Walter

6. Which painter does Fabio recommend?
   a. the first one
   b. the second one

Talk with a partner. Ask and answer the questions. Use complete sentences.

2 Grammar

A Write. Complete the conversation.

Rita: Saba, could you ____*help*____ me with something? My teacher is going to
1. help / helping

retire tomorrow, and I want to buy a gift _____ her. What should I get?
2. to / for

Saba: Would she _____ some flowers?
3. like / likes

Rita: Yes, she _____ . She loves flowers. Where can I buy them?
4. will / would

Saba: There's a small flower shop downtown, and a bigger one near the school.

Rita: _____ shop do you recommend?
5. Which / Where

Saba: I _____ the one near the school. It's cheaper.
6. like / likes

B Write. Look at the answers. Write the questions.

1. **A** What *does Rita want to buy for her teacher* ?

   B Rita wants to buy her teacher a gift.

2. **A** What _____ ?

   B Her teacher would like some flowers.

3. **A** Which _____ ?

   B Saba recommends the flower shop near the school.

Talk with a partner. Ask and answer the questions.

3 Pronunciation: the *-s* ending in the simple present

CLASS CD2 TK 36

A **Listen** to the *-s* ending in these simple present verbs.

/s/	/z/	/ɪz/
talks	is	watches
makes	has	fixes

CLASS CD2 TK 37

B **Listen and repeat.**

/s/	/z/	/ɪz/
wants	prefers	relaxes
suggests	recommends	teaches
unlocks	does	scratches

CLASS CD2 TK 38

C **Listen** and check (✓) the correct column.

Verb	/s/	/z/	/ɪz/	Verb	/s/	/z/	/ɪz/
1. drives				5. takes			
2. gets				6. wishes			
3. goes				7. sleeps			
4. uses				8. needs			

D **Write** six more verbs with *-s* endings in the simple present. Check (✓) the correct column for the pronunciation of the *-s* ending.

Verb	/s/	/z/	/ɪz/	Verb	/s/	/z/	/ɪz/
1.				4.			
2.				5.			
3.				6.			

Talk with a partner. Make a sentence with each word. Take turns.

Self-assessments

UNIT 1 Personal information

A Vocabulary Check (✓) the words you know.

- ☐ accessories
- ☐ belt
- ☐ checked
- ☐ curly
- ☐ dress
- ☐ long
- ☐ pants
- ☐ plaid
- ☐ shirt
- ☐ short
- ☐ skirt
- ☐ straight
- ☐ striped
- ☐ sunglasses
- ☐ uniform

B Skills and functions Read the sentences. Check (✓) what you know.

I can use adjectives in the correct order: *She's wearing a **black and white striped** shirt.*		I can look for key words to answer reading questions.	
I can use the present continuous: *What **are you doing** right now? **I'm reading**.*		I can write a paragraph describing a person.	
I can use the simple present: *What **does** he **do** every Saturday? He always **watches** TV.*		I can understand an order form.	
I can use **and . . . too** and **and . . . either** to show agreement and **but** to show differences: *Tam doesn't wear glasses, **and** I don't **either**. Silvia wears glasses, **but** I don't.*			

C What's next? Choose one.

☐ I am ready for the unit test.　　☐ I need more practice with _____.

UNIT 2 At school

A Vocabulary Check (✓) the words you know.

- ☐ computer lab
- ☐ criminal justice
- ☐ dental assisting
- ☐ fitness training
- ☐ goal
- ☐ home health care
- ☐ keyboard
- ☐ lab instructor
- ☐ nail care
- ☐ open a business
- ☐ veterinary assisting
- ☐ vocational course

B Skills and functions Read the sentences. Check (✓) what you know.

I can ask and answer questions using **want** and **need**: *What **do** they **want** to do? What **do** you **need** to do?*		I can read quickly to get the main idea.	
I can give advice about how to reach goals.		I can write about my goals.	
I can talk about the future using **will**: *What **will** she **do** on Tuesday? She**'ll** probably **go** to the movies.*		I can understand a course catalog.	
I can talk about the future using **be going to** or the present continuous: *He's **going to make** dinner tonight. He**'s making** dinner tonight.*			

C What's next? Choose one.

☐ I am ready for the unit test.　　☐ I need more practice with _____.

UNIT 3 Friends and family

A **Vocabulary** Check (✓) the words you know.

- ☐ broken down
- ☐ do the dishes
- ☐ do the laundry
- ☐ get dressed
- ☐ get up
- ☐ groceries
- ☐ make lunch
- ☐ make the bed
- ☐ overheated
- ☐ take a bath
- ☐ take a nap
- ☐ take a shower

B **Skills and functions** Read the sentences. Check (✓) what you know.

I can ask and answer questions using the simple past with regular and irregular verbs: *What **did** they **do** last night? They **went** to the movies and **listened** to music.*		I can write a journal entry about my day.	
I know when to use the simple present and when to use the simple past: *We usually **eat** dinner at 8:00. Yesterday, we **ate** dinner at 6:30.*		When I read, I can look for words that tell the order things happened.	
I can use expressions with ***make, do, play***, and ***go***: ***make** the bed, **do** the laundry, **play** cards, **go** dancing.*		I can understand cell phone calling plans.	
I can ask and answer questions about daily activities.			

C **What's next?** Choose one.

☐ I am ready for the unit test.   ☐ I need more practice with _____.

UNIT 4 Health

A **Vocabulary** Check (✓) the words you know.

- ☐ accident
- ☐ allergies
- ☐ chills
- ☐ crutches
- ☐ hurt
- ☐ injury
- ☐ prescription
- ☐ stiff neck
- ☐ swollen knee
- ☐ take medicine
- ☐ warning label
- ☐ X-ray

B **Skills and functions** Read the sentences. Check (✓) what you know.

I can ask and answer questions using ***should***: *What **should** they do? They **should** stay in the shade.*		I can read a warning label.	
I can ask and answer questions using ***have to***: *What **does** she **have to** do? She **has to** take her medicine.*		I can complete an accident report form.	
I can use ***must, must not, have to,*** and ***not have to*** to make statements: *You **must not drive** after you take it. You **don't have to take** it with food.*		I can understand a medicine label.	
I can talk about health problems.			

C **What's next?** Choose one.

☐ I am ready for the unit test.   ☐ I need more practice with _____.

UNIT 5 Around town

A **Vocabulary** Check (✓) the words you know.

☐ buy souvenirs	☐ never	☐ stay with relatives	☐ ticket booth
☐ go sightseeing	☐ rarely	☐ suitcase	☐ waiting area
☐ information desk	☐ sometimes	☐ take pictures	☐ write postcards

B **Skills and functions** Read the sentences. Check (✓) what you know.

I can ask and answer questions using **How often** and **How long**: **How often** does the train leave? Every 30 minutes. **How long** does it take? About three hours.		I can talk about travel activities.	
I can use adverbs of frequency: He **rarely** rides his bike. She **always** takes a taxi.		I can write a letter to a friend about a trip.	
I can give directions using **into**, **out of**, **through**, and **toward**: Walk **through** the tunnel. Go **toward** the exit.		I can understand an airline schedule.	
I can read a bus schedule.			

C **What's next?** Choose one.

☐ I am ready for the unit test.   ☐ I need more practice with _____.

UNIT 6 Time

A **Vocabulary** Check (✓) the words you know.

☐ become a citizen	☐ find a job	☐ get promoted	☐ immigrate
☐ citizenship exam	☐ get engaged	☐ graduate	☐ move
☐ fall in love	☐ get married	☐ have a baby	☐ retire

B **Skills and functions** Read the sentences. Check (✓) what you know.

I can ask and answer **When** questions to talk about the past: **When did** you **get married**? I **got married** in 1980.		I can make a time line.	
I can use time phrases: **three weeks ago, on Sunday, at 4:00 p.m., last year**.		I can write a paragraph about important events in my life.	
I can ask and answer questions with **someone**, **some**, **anyone**, **everyone**, and **no one**: Is **anyone** married? Yes, **everyone** is married. No, **no one** is married.		I can understand an application for a marriage license.	
I can talk about life events.			

C **What's next?** Choose one.

☐ I am ready for the unit test.   ☐ I need more practice with _____.

UNIT 7 Shopping

A Vocabulary Check (✓) the words you know.

- ☐ appliances
- ☐ aquarium
- ☐ cheap
- ☐ comfortable
- ☐ customer
- ☐ entertainment center
- ☐ expensive
- ☐ furniture
- ☐ gift
- ☐ heavy
- ☐ lamp
- ☐ mirror
- ☐ price tag
- ☐ sofa
- ☐ stove

B Skills and functions Read the sentences. Check (✓) what you know.

I can use comparatives: **bigger**, **cheaper**, **heavier**, **more expensive**.		I can guess the meaning of new words from other words nearby.	
I can use superlatives: **the biggest, the cheapest, the heaviest, the most expensive**.		I can write about the best gift I ever received.	
I can use **one**, **the other**, **some**, and **the others** to replace nouns: *There are two clothing stores.* **One** *sells men's clothing.* **The other** *sells women's clothing.*		I can understand a sales receipt.	
I can talk about furniture.			

C What's next? Choose one.

☐ I am ready for the unit test.   ☐ I need more practice with _____.

UNIT 8 Work

A Vocabulary Check (✓) the words you know.

- ☐ assist
- ☐ clear tables
- ☐ co-workers
- ☐ deliver
- ☐ handle money
- ☐ job duties
- ☐ lab
- ☐ linens
- ☐ orderly
- ☐ patient
- ☐ pick up
- ☐ prepare
- ☐ supplies
- ☐ walker
- ☐ wheelchair

B Skills and functions Read the sentences. Check (✓) what you know.

I can ask and answer **Where** and **What** questions in the simple past: **What did** he do? **Where did** you **go**?		I can talk about job duties.	
I can use the conjunctions **and**, **or**, and **but**: *She wrote reports* **and** *checked e-mail. She can write reports* **or** *check e-mail. She wrote reports,* **but** *she didn't check e-mail.*		I can write about my employment history.	
I can use **could**, **couldn't**, **can**, and **can't** to talk about past and present ability: *I* **couldn't** *drive a car before, but I* **can** *drive a car now.*		I can scan a text for specific information (names, dates).	
I can read and understand a letter of recommendation.		I can understand a weekly time sheet.	

C What's next? Choose one.

☐ I am ready for the unit test.   ☐ I need more practice with _____.

UNIT 9 Daily living

Vocabulary Check (✓) the words you know.

☐ clogged	☐ fix	☐ a leak	☐ plumber	☐ a sink
☐ a dryer	☐ garbage	☐ a lightbulb	☐ recommend	☐ tenant
☐ electrician	☐ jammed	☐ a lock	☐ repair	☐ unclog

B **Skills and functions** Read the sentences. Check (✓) what you know.

I can make requests using **Can**, **Could**, **Will**, and **Would**: **Could** you clean the bathroom, please?		I can talk about problems in a home or an apartment.	
I can ask **Which** questions using the simple present: **Which** electrician do you recommend?		I can write a letter of complaint to a building manager or landlord.	
I can make suggestions using **Let's** and **Let's not**: **Let's** buy a refrigerator. **Let's not** paint.		I can understand an invoice.	
I can read a notice to tenants.			

C **What's next?** Choose one.

☐ I am ready for the unit test.   ☐ I need more practice with _____.

UNIT 10 Free time

A **Vocabulary** Check (✓) the words you know.

☐ baby shower	☐ card	☐ graduation party	☐ present
☐ balloons	☐ celebrate	☐ housewarming	☐ thank-you note
☐ cake	☐ flowers	☐ invitation	☐ wedding

B **Skills and functions** Read the sentences. Check (✓) what you know.

I can ask and answer questions with **Would you like . . . ?**: **Would you like** a cup of coffee? Yes, **I would**.		I can look for examples of the main idea in a paragraph.	
I can make statements with direct and indirect objects: I gave **her some books**.		I can read and write a thank-you note.	
I can use **there is** / **there are** and **there was** / **there were** to talk about the present and past.		I can understand an invitation to a party.	
I can talk about celebrations.			

C **What's next?** Choose one.

☐ I am ready for the unit test.   ☐ I need more practice with _____.

Reference

Present continuous

Use the present continuous for actions happening now and in the near future.

Wh- questions

What	am	I	doing now?
	are	you	
	is	he	
	is	she	
	is	it	
	are	we	
	are	you	
	are	they	

Answers

You're	working.
I'm	
He's	
She's	
It's	
You're	
We're	
They're	

Contractions

I'm	=	I am
You're	=	You are
He's	=	He is
She's	=	She is
It's	=	It is
We're	=	We are
You're	=	You are
They're	=	They are

Simple present

Use the simple present for repeated, usual, or daily actions.

Yes / No questions

Do	I	work?
Do	you	
Does	he	
Does	she	
Does	it	
Do	we	
Do	you	
Do	they	

Short answers

Yes,	you	do.		No,	you	don't.
	I	do.			I	don't.
	he	does.			he	doesn't.
	she	does.			she	doesn't.
	it	does.			it	doesn't.
	you	do.			you	don't.
	we	do.			we	don't.
	they	do.			they	don't.

Wh- questions: *What*

What	do	I	do every day?
	do	you	
	does	he	
	does	she	
	does	it	
	do	we	
	do	you	
	do	they	

Answers

You	usually	work.
I		work.
He		works.
She		works.
It		works.
You		work.
We		work.
They		work.

Wh- questions: *When*

When	do	I	usually work?
	do	you	
	does	he	
	does	she	
	do	we	
	do	you	
	do	they	

Answers

You	usually	work	on Friday.
I		work	
He		works	
She		works	
You		work	
We		work	
They		work	

Simple present of *want* and *need*

Wh- questions: *What*

	do	I		
	do	you		
	does	he		
What	does	she	want	to do?
	do	we		
	do	you		
	do	they		
	do	I		
	do	you		
	does	he		
What	does	she	need	to do?
	do	we		
	do	you		
	do	they		

Answers

You	want	
I	want	
He	wants	
She	wants	to go home.
You	want	
We	want	
They	want	
You	need	
I	need	
He	needs	
She	needs	to go home.
You	need	
We	need	
They	need	

Simple present of *have to* + verb

Wh- questions: *What*

	do	I		
	do	you		
	does	he		
What	does	she	have to	do?
	does	it		
	do	we		
	do	you		
	do	they		

Answers

You	have to	
I	have to	
He	has to	
She	has to	go home.
It	has to	
You	have to	
We	have to	
They	have to	

Simple present with *Which* questions

Wh- questions: *Which*

	do	I	
	do	you	
	does	he	
Which plumber	does	she	recommend?
	does	it	
	do	we	
	do	you	
	do	they	

Answers

You	recommend	
I	recommend	
He	recommends	
She	recommends	Joe's Plumbing.
It	recommends	
You	recommend	
We	recommend	
They	recommend	

Simple past with regular and irregular verbs

Use the simple past for actions completed in the past.

Wh- questions: *What*

What	did	I	do?
		you	
		he	
		she	
		it	
		we	
		you	
		they	

Affirmative statements

I	
You	
He	
She	stayed. / ate.
It	
We	
You	
They	

Negative statements

I		
You		
He		
She	didn't	stay. / eat.
It		
We		
You		
They		

didn't = did not

Yes / No questions

Did	I	stay? / eat?
	you	
	he	
	she	
	it	
	we	
	you	
	they	

Short answers

Yes,	you	did.
	I	
	he	
	she	
	it	
	you	
	we	
	they	

No,	you	didn't.
	I	
	he	
	she	
	it	
	you	
	we	
	they	

Wh- questions: *When*

When	did	I	move? / leave?
		you	
		he	
		she	
		it	
		we	
		you	
		they	

Answers

You		
I		
He		
She	moved / left	last week.
It		
You		
We		
They		

Wh- questions: *Where*

Where	did	I	go?
		you	
		he	
		she	
		it	
		we	
		you	
		they	

Answers

You		
I		
He		
She	stayed / went	home.
It		
You		
We		
They		

Future with *will*

Use *will* for a prediction or promise in the future.

Wh- questions: *What*

What	will	I	do	tomorrow?
		you		
		he		
		she		
		we		
		you		
		they		

Affirmative statements

I'll		
You'll		
He'll		
She'll	probably	work.
We'll		
You'll		
They'll		

'll = will

Negative statements

I		
You		
He		
She	won't	work.
We		
You		
They		

won't = will not

Future with *be going to*

Use *be going to* for a plan or prediction in the future.

Wh- questions

What	am	I	going to do tomorrow?
	are	you	
	is	he	
	is	she	
	are	we	
	are	you	
	are	they	

Affirmative statements

I'm		
You're		
He's		
She's	going to	play soccer.
We're		
You're		
They're		

Negative statements

I'm		
You're		
He's		
She's	not going to	play soccer.
We're		
You're		
They're		

Should

Wh- questions: *What*

What	should	I	do?
		you	
		he	
		she	
		we	
		you	
		they	

Affirmative statements

I		
You		
He		
She	should	take medicine.
We		
You		
They		

Negative statements

I		
You		
He		
She	shouldn't	take medicine.
We		
You		
They		

shouldn't = should not

Would you like . . . ?

Yes / No questions

Would	you / he / she / you / they	like	some cake?

Short answers

Yes,	I / he / she / we / they	would.

Wh- questions: What

What	would	you / he / she / you / they	like?

Answers

I'd / He'd / She'd / We'd / They'd	like	some cake.

'd = would

Direct and indirect objects

Tim gave a present to	me. / you. / him. / her. / Mary. / it. / us. / you. / them.

Tim gave	me / you / him / her / Mary / it / us / you / them	a present.

Simple past irregular verbs

be	→ was / were	eat	→ ate	know	→ knew	sit	→ sat
become	→ became	fall	→ fell	leave	→ left	sleep	→ slept
begin	→ began	feel	→ felt	lose	→ lost	speak	→ spoke
break	→ broke	fight	→ fought	make	→ made	spend	→ spent
bring	→ brought	find	→ found	meet	→ met	stand	→ stood
build	→ built	fly	→ flew	pay	→ paid	steal	→ stole
buy	→ bought	forget	→ forgot	put	→ put	swim	→ swam
catch	→ caught	give	→ gave	read	→ read	take	→ took
choose	→ chose	go	→ went	ride	→ rode	teach	→ taught
come	→ came	have	→ had	run	→ ran	tell	→ told
cost	→ cost	hear	→ heard	say	→ said	think	→ thought
cut	→ cut	hide	→ hid	see	→ saw	understand	→ understood
do	→ did	hold	→ held	sell	→ sold	wake	→ woke
drink	→ drank	hurt	→ hurt	send	→ sent	wear	→ wore
drive	→ drove	keep	→ kept	sing	→ sang	write	→ wrote

Comparative and superlative adjectives

	Adjective	Comparative	Superlative
Adjectives with one syllable	cheap large long new nice old short small tall young	cheaper larger longer newer nicer older shorter smaller taller younger	the cheapest the largest the longest the newest the nicest the oldest the shortest the smallest the tallest the youngest
Adjectives with one syllable ending in a vowel-consonant pair	big fat hot sad	bigger fatter hotter sadder	the biggest the fattest the hottest the saddest
Adjectives with two or more syllables	beautiful comfortable crowded expensive	more beautiful more comfortable more crowded more expensive	the most beautiful the most comfortable the most crowded the most expensive
Adjectives ending in -y	friendly heavy pretty	friendlier heavier prettier	the friendliest the heaviest the prettiest
Irregular adjectives	good bad	better worse	the best the worst

Adjective word order

Size	Age	Shape	Color	Pattern
big large long medium short small	modern new old	curly oval round square straight	black blue brown green purple red white yellow	checked plaid polka dotted striped

Examples

He's wearing a modern purple and yellow striped tie.
She has a large square brown coffee table.
They have a medium-sized old green car.

Ordinal numbers

1st first	11th eleventh	21st twenty-first	31st thirty-first
2nd second	12th twelfth	22nd twenty-second	
3rd third	13th thirteenth	23rd twenty-third	
4th fourth	14th fourteenth	24th twenty-fourth	
5th fifth	15th fifteenth	25th twenty-fifth	
6th sixth	16th sixteenth	26th twenty-sixth	
7th seventh	17th seventeenth	27th twenty-seventh	
8th eighth	18th eighteenth	28th twenty-eighth	
9th ninth	19th nineteenth	29th twenty-ninth	
10th tenth	20th twentieth	30th thirtieth	

Metric equivalents

1 inch = 25 millimeters	1 dry ounce = 28 grams	1 fluid ounce = 30 milliliters
1 foot = 30 centimeters	1 pound = .45 kilograms	1 quart = .95 liters
1 yard = .9 meters	1 mile = 1.6 kilometers	1 gallon = 3.8 liters

Converting Fahrenheit temperatures to Celsius

Subtract 30 and divide by 2.
Example: 80°F − 30 = 50; 50 divided by 2 = 25
80°F = approximately 25°C

Spelling rules

Comparative adjectives
- For adjectives with one syllable, add -er or -r:

  old → older   nice → nicer
- For adjectives with one syllable ending in a vowel-consonant pair, double the consonant and add -er:

  big → bigger
- For adjectives with two or more syllables, add more:

  expensive → more expensive
- For adjectives ending in -y, change y to i and add -er:

  pretty → prettier

Superlative adjectives
- For adjectives with one syllable, add the before the adjective and add -est or -st:

  old → the oldest   nice → the nicest
- For adjectives with one syllable ending in a vowel-consonant pair, add the, double the consonant, and add -est:

  big → the biggest
- For adjectives with two or more syllables, add the most:

  expensive → the most expensive
- For adjectives ending in -y, add the, change y to i, and add -est:

  pretty → the prettiest

Punctuation rules

- Sentences can end with a period (.), question mark (?), or exclamation point (!):

  Simple statement: *We have cookies.*

  Question: *Do we have cookies?*

  Strong feeling: *We have cookies!*

- Put a comma (,) after every item when a list has three or more items:

  We have soda, coffee, and water.

- Use a comma (,) after time phrases like *After class, On the weekend, In 2001,* or *On July 4th* when they come at the beginning of a sentence.

- Use a comma (,) after sequence words:

  First, I washed the dirty clothes.

- Begin paragraphs with an indent (space).

- Begin a new paragraph when you start a new topic or change the tense (time).

- Indent the paragraphs in an informal note. Don't indent the date or *Dear* _____ .

Capitalization rules

Use capital letters for clothing sizes.	**XS** (extra small) **S** (small) **M** (medium) **L** (large) **XL** (extra large)
Begin names of departments with a capital letter.	**L**ost and **F**ound **H**uman **R**esources **D**epartment
Use capital letters for abbreviations.	**D.C.** (District of Columbia)
Begin titles with a capital letter when they follow a name in a letter.	**S**tella **T**aylor **C**hairperson **T**enants' **C**ommittee

Map of North America

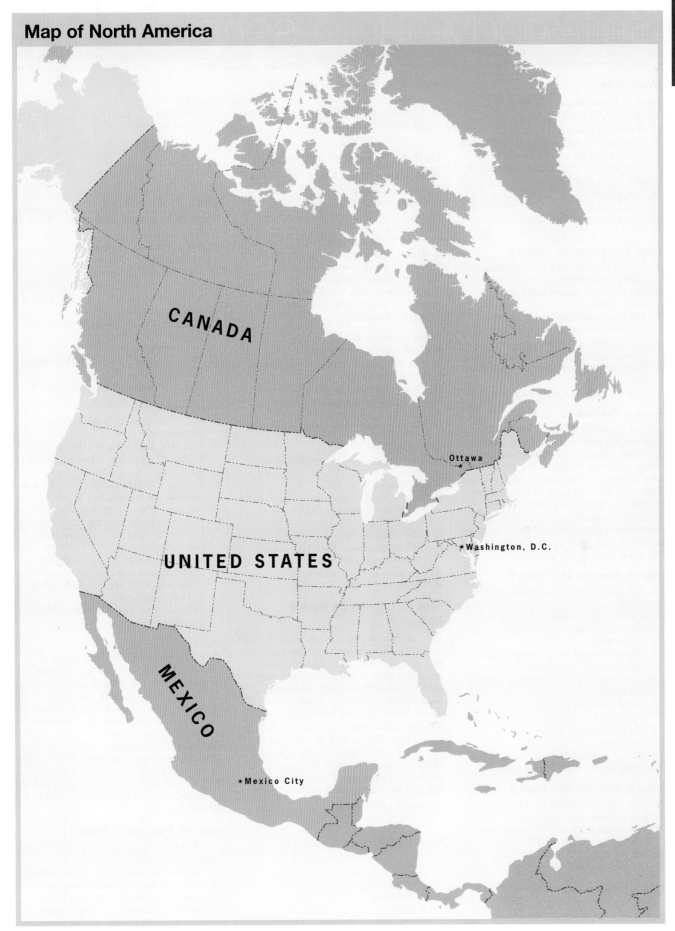

CANADA

★ Ottawa

UNITED STATES

★ Washington, D.C.

MEXICO

★ Mexico City

Self-study audio script

Welcome

Page 3, Exercise 2A – Track 2

A Hi. I'm looking for a job.
B What can you do?
A I can use a computer very well. I can speak English and Spanish. I can help students with their homework, and I can read to children.
B Can you write in English?
A Yes, I can.
B Can you speak Russian?
A No, I can't. But I'm going to learn.

Page 4, Exercise 3A – Track 3

1. I am a student at Preston Adult Learning Center.
2. My English classes are very interesting.
3. My classmates are from many different countries.
4. My teacher is from Canada.
5. Maria and Gricela are from Peru.
6. They were in my class last semester, too.
7. The teacher was Ms. Gonzalez.

Page 4, Exercise 3B – Track 4

My name is Maria. I am from Mexico. My husband's name is Sergio. He's from Mexico, too. There are three children in our family – one son and two daughters. Our son, Javier, is seven years old. He was born in Mexico. Our daughters, Melisa and Maritza, are twins. They are four years old. They were born in the United States. Sergio and I weren't born in the United States. We were born in Mexico.

Page 5, Exercise 4A – Track 5

1. Bao takes out the garbage every week.
2. I work at a restaurant every day.
3. Eva visited her parents in the afternoon.
4. We celebrated my parents' fiftieth anniversary last night.
5. Sarah went to the baseball game yesterday.
6. Mike took the bus last week.
7. She didn't buy candy yesterday.
8. He wants to go to the mall on Saturday.
9. Akiko sleeps late on Sundays.
10. They don't usually walk to school.

Page 5, Exercise 4B – Track 6

A When did you come to this country?
B I came here two years ago.
A You speak very well. Did you study English here last year?
B Yes, I did.
A Did you speak English in your native country?
B No, I didn't.

A What do you usually do on the weekend?
B I usually stay home, but sometimes I go shopping.

Unit 1: Personal information

Page 7, Exercises 2A and 2B – Track 7

Conversation A
A Shoko, who's this?
B This is a picture of my daughter, Victoria.
A What's she wearing?
B Her soccer uniform. She plays every day. She's very athletic.
A Wow! She's really tall.
B Yes, she is. She looks like her father.
A She's a pretty girl. Her long black hair is beautiful.

Conversation B
A Shoko, is that your son?
B Yes. This is my teenage son, Eddie.
A What's he doing?
B He's playing computer games. He always plays computer games!
A Does he have a lot of friends?
B No, not many. He's a very quiet boy.

Conversation C
B This is a picture of my husband, Mark.
A Oh, Shoko, he *is* tall!
B Yes, he is. He wears very large shirts and pants. I buy his clothes at a special store.
A What does he do?
B He's an engineer. He's very smart. He studies English, too.
A You have a really nice family.
B Thanks.

Page 12, Exercise 2 – Track 8

Hi Karin,

How are you doing? Guess what! Today is my daughter's birthday. The last time you saw Victoria, she was three years old. Now she's 17! She's tall and very athletic. She likes sports. She plays soccer every afternoon. Here is her photo. She's wearing her red and white striped soccer uniform. She usually wears jeans and a T-shirt. Victoria is also a very good student. She has lots of friends and goes with them to the mall every weekend. How are your daughters? Please send a photo!

Let's stay in touch.

Shoko

Page 13, Exercise 4A – Track 9

1. a hat
2. a tie
3. a watch
4. sunglasses
5. a scarf

6. gloves
7. a purse
8. earrings
9. a necklace
10. a bracelet
11. a belt
12. a ring

Unit 2: At school

Page 19, Exercises 2A and 2B – Track 10

Conversation A
A Oh, what's wrong with this computer!
B Um, Joseph, do you need help?
A Oh, thanks, Eva. I'm having trouble with this keyboard. I need to take a computer class.
B Ask the teacher about keyboarding classes. She helped me find a citizenship class.
A That's a great idea. I'll talk to Mrs. Lee after class. Thanks!
B You're welcome, Joseph. Good luck!

Conversation B
C Oh, hi, Joseph. Do you need something?
A Yes, Mrs. Lee. I want to learn keyboarding skills. What do I need to do?
C Hmm . . . keyboarding skills. Do you need to use a computer at work?
A No, not right now. But someday I want to open my own business. I'm pretty sure I'll need to use a computer then.
C Well, you can study keyboarding in the computer lab across the hall. You could talk with Mr. Stephens. He's the lab instructor.
A Thanks, Mrs. Lee. I'll talk to Mr. Stephens right now.

Conversation C
A Hello, Mr. Stephens. My name is Joseph. Mrs. Lee told me to come here. I want to learn keyboarding.
D That's great. You can join my keyboarding class. First, you need to register with Mrs. Smith in the Registration Office.
A Great. I'll go register now.
D But there's one problem.
A One problem?
D Yes. The Registration Office is closed today. You can register next week.
A OK. Thanks.

Page 24, Exercise 2 – Track 11

What are your future goals? What steps do you need to take?

I want to open my own electronics store. I need to take three steps to reach my goal. First, I need to learn keyboarding. Second, I need to take business classes. Third, I need to work in an electronics store. I will probably open my store in a couple of years.

Page 25, Exercise 4A – Track 12
1. home health care
2. counseling
3. veterinary assisting
4. physical therapy assisting
5. criminal justice
6. fitness training
7. dental assisting
8. nail care
9. computer networking

Unit 3: Friends and family
Page 33, Exercises 2A and 2B – Track 13
Conversation A
A Rigatoni Restaurant. Daniel speaking.
B Hi, Daniel? It's me.
A Rosa? Hi. Is everything OK?
B Not really. I went to the supermarket with the children, and the car broke down.
A The car broke down! What's wrong?
B I don't know. I think it's the engine.
A Did you open the hood?
B Yes, I did. There's a lot of smoke!
A Where are you?
B I'm at the side of the road near the supermarket.
A Stay there. I'm going to leave work right now. I'll be there in ten minutes.
B OK. I have a lot of groceries in the trunk. Please hurry.

Conversation B
C Mike's Auto Repair.
B Hi, Mike, It's Rosa – Daniel's wife?
C Oh, hi, Rosa. How are you?
B Well, not so good.
C Why? What's wrong?
B Well, this morning I went to the store to buy groceries for a picnic, but then our car broke down. My husband came and picked us up.
C Oh, I'm sorry, Rosa.
B Could you pick up the car for us? It's on the side of the road near the supermarket.
C Of course. I'll pick it up and take it to my shop this afternoon.
B Thanks, Mike.

Conversation C
D Hello, Swift Dry Cleaner's.
B Hi, Ling. It's Rosa. How are you?
D I'm good. I'm almost done with work. Will I see you tonight?
B I'm not sure. We had car trouble today. I need a ride to school tonight. Can you pick me up?
D Sure. What time?
B I usually leave my house at 7 o'clock.
D Ok. I'll pick you up at 7.
B That's great. You're a good friend, Ling. Thank you.
D No problem. See you tonight.

Page 38, Exercise 2 – Track 14
Thursday, June 20th
    Today was a bad day! On Thursday, my children and I usually go to the park for a picnic, but today we had a problem. We drove to the store to buy groceries, and then the car broke down. I checked the engine, and there was a lot of smoke. I think the engine overheated. Luckily, I had my cell phone! First, I called my husband at work. He left early, picked us up, and took us home. Next, I called the mechanic. Finally, I called Ling and asked for a ride to school tonight. In the end, we didn't go to the park because it was too late. Instead, we had a picnic in our backyard. Then, Ling drove me to school.

Page 39, Exercise 4A – Track 15
1. make lunch
2. take a bath
3. do the dishes
4. do the laundry
5. get up
6. do homework
7. take a nap
8. make the bed
9. get dressed

Unit 4: Health
Page 45, Exercises 2A and 2B – Track 16
Conversation A
A Hello?
B Lily, it's me. I had a little accident.
A Are you OK, Hamid? What happened?
B I fell off a ladder at work. I hurt my leg.
A Hamid, you should go to the hospital!
B I'm at the hospital now. But listen, you have to pick up the children at school. I have to wait for the doctor.
A OK, I'll pick up the children. I'll see you back at home.
B OK, thanks, Lily. Bye.

Conversation B
C Hello?
B Chris, it's Hamid.
C Hey, how's it going?
B Not so good. I had a little accident at work. I fell off a ladder.
C Oh, no. Are you OK?
B Well, I hurt my leg. I'm at the hospital now, and I had to get an X-ray. Could you come to the hospital and drive me home?
C Of course. What's the address?
B It's 3560 East 54th Street. You should take the highway.
C OK, I'm leaving right now.
B Thanks, Chris. Bye.

Conversation C
D Ace Construction.
B Hi, Angie. It's Hamid. I need to talk to Mr. Jackson, please.
D Hi, Hamid. Just a second.

E Hi, Hamid. Jackson here. How's it going? Did you finish painting the house on Main Street?
B Well, no. I had a little accident. I slipped and fell off the ladder. I'm at the hospital now.
E Oh, no! Are you badly hurt?
B I don't know. I had to get an X-ray of my leg. The doctor is looking at the X-ray now.
E Hamid, you have to fill out an accident report. Call me after you see the doctor.
B OK. What about the paint job?
E Don't worry. Felipe will finish it. Stay home tomorrow. You should rest.
B OK. Thanks, Mr. Jackson. Bye.

Page 50, Exercise 2 – Track 17
WARNING: PREVENT ACCIDENTS. READ BEFORE USING!
    Face the ladder when climbing up and down.
    Don't carry a lot of equipment while climbing a ladder – wear a tool belt.
    Never stand on the shelf of the ladder – stand on the steps.
    Never stand on the top step of a ladder.
    Be safe! Always read and follow the safety stickers.

Page 51, Exercise 4A – Track 18
1. a swollen knee
2. a sprained wrist
3. chest pains
4. high blood pressure
5. allergies
6. chills
7. a bad cut
8. a rash
9. a stiff neck

Unit 5: Around town
Page 59, Exercises 2A and 2B – Track 19
Conversation A
A Attention, please. This is an announcement.
B What's that, Binh?
C That's just an announcement, Mom. The announcer is giving train information. We should listen.
A Trains to Boston leave every hour. The next train to Boston will leave at 7:20 from Track 1. I repeat. The next train to Boston will leave at 7:20 from Track 1.
B That was about trains to Boston. We need information about trains to New York.
C Wait. Here's another announcement.
A Trains to New York City leave every . . . The next train to New York will leave at . . . I repeat. The next train to New York will leave at . . . from Track 2.
B Oh, no! We didn't hear the information about New York!

Conversation B

B There's an information desk over there. You can ask about trains from Philadelphia to New York.

C Oh, good. Excuse me. I need some train information.

D How can I help you?

C I'm taking my mother to New York City today. How often do trains go to New York?

D Trains leave for New York every 30 minutes.

C When does the next train leave for New York?

D The 7:05 train just left. The next train leaves at 7:35 from Track 3.

C Thanks.

D Do you have tickets? You can get them at the ticket booth over there.

C No, we don't have tickets. Thank you very much.

Conversation C

C I got our tickets, Mom. Our train leaves in 25 minutes.

B Good. We don't have to wait long.

C Do you want to sit down? We can sit in the waiting area.

B That's a good idea. My suitcase is heavy. This train station is beautiful.

C Yeah, it really is. I always travel by train. It's a lot easier than driving.

B How long does it take to drive to New York?

C It usually takes about 2 hours to drive. It takes less than one and a half hours by train.

A Attention, please. The train to New York is now boarding on Track 3.

C That's our train, Mom. Let's go!

Page 64, Exercise 2 – Track 20

Dear Layla,

Right now, my mother is visiting me here in Philadelphia. I rarely see her because she comes to Philadelphia only once a year. She usually stays for one month. Here is a photo of my mother at the airport last week. She was happy to see me!

This year, I want to take my mother to New York City. I want to show her the Statue of Liberty and Central Park. It takes about one and a half hours to get to New York by train. We are excited about our trip. Can you meet us there? Let me know.

Your friend,
Binh

Page 65, Exercise 4A – Track 21

1. write postcards
2. stay at a hotel
3. take a suitcase
4. buy souvenirs
5. go swimming
6. stay with relatives
7. take pictures
8. go shopping
9. go sightseeing

Unit 6: Time

Page 71, Exercises 2A and 2B – Track 22

Conversation A

A Olga, I love your new apartment.

B Thanks, Victoria. We moved in two months ago. You're our first visitor.

A Is that your wedding picture?

B Yes, it is. That's my husband and me a long time ago.

A What a good-looking bride and groom! When did you get married?

B Let's see. We got married in 1990.

A You were young! My husband and I had our third wedding anniversary last month. Do you have more pictures?

B Sure. They're in our photo album. Do you want to see them?

A I'd love to.

Conversation B

A Your pictures are wonderful. You have a lovely family.

B Thanks!

A How old are your children?

B My son, Sergey, is 19 now. His birthday was three days ago. He started college in September.

A When did your daughter start college?

B Start college? Natalya's only 14!

A Wow! She's tall for her age.

B Yes, she is. She started high school on Tuesday.

Conversation C

A Is that a picture of Russia?

B Yes. That's in Moscow.

A Did you live in Moscow?

B Yes. We met in Moscow. We went to school there before we got married.

A It looks like an interesting city.

B Oh, it is!

A When did you move to the United States?

B We moved here about 14 years ago.

A Were your children born here?

B Natalya was. Sergey was born in Russia, like us.

Page 76, Exercise 2 – Track 23

An Interesting Life

A What happened after you graduated from high school?

B I went to university in Moscow, and I met my husband there. It was a long time ago! We were in the same class. We fell in love and got married on April 2nd, 1990. We had a small wedding in Moscow.

A What happened after you got married?

B I finished university and found a job. I was a teacher. Then, I had a baby. My husband and I were very excited to have a little boy.

A When did you move to the United States?

B We immigrated about 14 years ago. We became American citizens eight years ago.

Page 77, Exercise 4A – Track 24

1. retired
2. started a business
3. had a baby
4. fell in love
5. got engaged
6. got married
7. got divorced
8. immigrated
9. got promoted

Unit 7: Shopping

Page 85, Exercises 2A and 2B – Track 25

Conversation A

A Good afternoon, folks. I'm Mike. How can I help you?

B Hi, I'm Denise. This is my husband, Nick. We need some furniture.

C A lot of furniture!

B We bought a house two days ago.

A Congratulations! This is the right place for furniture and appliances. We're having our biggest sale of the year. All our furniture is marked down 20 percent.

B Wow! 20 percent.

A We have chairs, lamps, sofas. . . . Look around. We have the best prices in town.

B Are the appliances 20 percent off, too?

A Yes! Refrigerators, stoves – everything in the store is 20 percent off.

C Thanks.

Conversation B

B Nick, look at that sofa. It's very pretty!

C Which one? The brown one?

B No, not the brown one, the blue one. It looks nice and comfortable. I like it.

C Hmm. But the brown sofa is bigger. I want a big sofa.

B Well, it is bigger, but look at the price, Nick. It's much more expensive than the blue sofa.

C Whoa! A thousand dollars? That's crazy!

B Look, there are some more sofas over there. Maybe they're cheaper.

C I sure hope so.

Conversation C

B Oh, look, Nick. They have pianos for sale.

C Pianos? But we aren't looking for a piano. We're looking for a sofa.

B I love this piano. Excuse me, miss? Do you work here?

D Yes. My name is Tara. How can I help you?

B Could you tell me about this piano?

D Oh, the upright piano? It's very old, but it's the most beautiful piano in the store. It also has a beautiful sound. Listen.

B Wow! Is it expensive?

D Well, it's $960. This small piano is cheaper, but the sound isn't the same.

B The upright piano is better. Let's buy it, Nick!

C Hey, not so fast! We came here to buy a sofa, not a piano!

Page 90, Exercise 2 – Track 26

Today's Question

What's the best thing you ever bought?

The best thing I ever bought was an old piano. I bought it in a used-furniture store last month. It was the most beautiful piano in the store, but it wasn't very expensive. It has a beautiful sound. Now my two children are taking piano lessons. I love to hear music in the house.

Denise Robinson – Charleston, South Carolina

I bought a used van five years ago. I used my van to help people move and to deliver stoves and refrigerators from a secondhand appliance store. I made a lot of money with that van. Now I have my own business. That van is the best thing I ever bought.

Sammy Chin – Myrtle Beach, South Carolina

Page 91, Exercise 4A – Track 27

1. aquarium
2. computer desk
3. mirror
4. end table
5. sofa bed
6. bookcase
7. entertainment center
8. coffee table
9. recliner

Unit 8: Work

Page 97, Exercises 2A and 2B – Track 28

Conversation A

A Hey, Marco. How are you?

B Oh, hi, Arlen. I'm fine. I had a busy day today.

A What did you do?

B Hmm . . . let's see. This morning, I delivered flowers to patients and picked up X-rays from the lab. I also delivered clean linens to the third floor. This afternoon, I made the beds on the second floor and prepared the rooms. And now I'm delivering supplies.

A Wow! You did have a busy day!

Conversation B

B Hi, John. How's it going?

C Hi, Marco. I'm tired. I worked the night shift last night.

B Oh, no.

C I like this job, but I don't like the night shift.

B I like this job, too, but I don't like the pay. I'm thinking about going back to school.

C Really? School is expensive.

B I know. Maybe I can find a part-time job and go to school full-time.

C Maybe you can work here part-time. You should ask about it.

Conversation C

B Is this the HR Office? Human Resources?

D Yes, come on in. I'm Suzanne Briggs. I'm the HR Assistant.

B Hi, Suzanne. I'm Marco Alba. I'm an orderly here.

D Hi, Marco. Have a seat. How can I help you?

B I like my job here, but I don't want to be an orderly forever. I want to go to nursing school and become a nurse.

D A nurse? That's great, Marco!

B I want to go to nursing school full-time and work part-time.

D That's a great idea! A lot of employees do that.

B Can I work part-time here at Valley Hospital?

D I don't know. Can you come back tomorrow? I'll find out about part-time jobs for you.

B Sure. Thanks, Suzanne. See you tomorrow.

Page 102, Exercise 2 – Track 29

Dear Mr. O'Hara:

I am happy to write this letter of recommendation for Marco Alba. Marco started working at Valley Hospital as an orderly in 2007. He takes patients from their rooms to the lab, delivers X-rays, and takes flowers and mail to patients. He also delivers linens and supplies. He is an excellent worker, and his co-workers like him very much.

We are sorry to lose Marco. He wants to go to school and needs to work part-time, but we don't have a part-time job for him right now. I recommend Marco very highly. Please contact me for more information.

Sincerely,

Suzanne Briggs

Human Resources Assistant

Page 103, Exercise 4A – Track 30

1. repair cars
2. operate large machines
3. clear tables
4. prepare food
5. help the nurses
6. take care of a family
7. handle money
8. assist the pharmacist
9. assist the doctor

Unit 9: Daily living

Page 111, Exercises 2A and 2B – Track 31

Conversation A

A Hello, Building Manager.

B Hi, this is Stella Taylor in Apartment 4B. I've got a problem. The washing machine overflowed. And the dishwasher's leaking, too. And the

sink is clogged. Could you please recommend a plumber?

A Well, I usually use two different plumbers.

B Which one do you recommend?

A Let's see. His name is Don Brown. He has a company on Main Street. Here's the phone number: 555-4564. He's really good.

B Thanks. I'll call him right away.

Conversation B

C Brown's Plumbing Service, Martha speaking. May I help you?

B I hope so. My washing machine overflowed, and my dishwasher is leaking all over the floor, and my sink is clogged. May I speak to Don Brown, please?

C Oh, Don's out right now on a job. But he'll be finished in an hour. He can come then. Can you wait an hour?

B One hour? Hmm. I need to go to work soon. Maybe my neighbor can unlock the door for him. My address is 3914 Fifth Street, Apartment 4B.

C OK. He'll be there in an hour.

B Thank you.

Conversation C

D Russell Taylor speaking.

B Hi, Russell. It's me. I have bad news. The washing machine overflowed, and the dishwasher is leaking on the floor, and the sink is clogged!

D Oh, no. Look, I'm really busy at work right now. Could you please call a plumber?

B I already did.

D You did? Which plumber did you call?

B Brown's Plumbing Service. The plumber will be here in an hour.

D But you're going to work.

B It's OK. I asked Mrs. Lee to let him in.

D All right, Stella. I'll see you tonight.

Page 116, Exercise 2 – Track 32

Attention, tenants:

Do you have problems in your apartment? Is anyone fixing them?

- Many tenants have broken windows.
- Tenants on the third floor have no lights in the hall.
- A tenant on the second floor has a leaking ceiling.
- Tenants on the first floor smell garbage every day.
- I'm really upset! We need to get together and write a letter of complaint to the manager of the building.

Come to a meeting Friday night at 7 p.m. in Apartment 4B.

Stella Taylor, Tenant 4B.

Page 117, Exercise 4A – Track 33

1. broken
2. dripping
3. torn
4. scratched
5. bent

6. burned out
7. cracked
8. stained
9. jammed

Unit 10: Free time

Page 123, Exercises 2A and 2B – Track 34

Conversation A

A Aunt Ana! Hello!
B Hi, Celia. Congratulations on your graduation! This is a wonderful party!
A Thank you for coming. Would you like some cake? My mother made it.
B I'd love some. I'm very hungry.
A Would you like something to drink?
B No, thanks. Here. I brought you some flowers. They're from my garden.
A Red roses! They're beautiful! Thank you.

Conversation B

A Hello, Mrs. Campbell. Thank you for coming to my party.
C Celia, I'm so proud of you. You were my best student. You started English class three years ago, and now you have your GED! You worked very hard.
A Thank you, Mrs. Campbell. You helped me a lot.
C Here. I brought you a card.
A Oh, thank you! Oh, that's so nice. Thank you, Mrs. Campbell.
C You're welcome.
A Come and join the party. Would you like a piece of cake?
C Yes, please. I'd love some.

Conversation C

A Hi, Sue. Thanks for coming. Where are your children?
D They're with my mother, so I can't stay long. I just wanted to congratulate you.
A Thank you. Would you like a piece of cake?
D No, thanks. I'm not hungry.
A Would you like something to drink?
D I'd love some water.
A OK. I'll get you some.
D Wait. I brought you a little present.
A Oh, thank you! Oh, Sue! My favorite perfume! Thank you!
D You're welcome. It's from our family.
A That's so nice. Please take some balloons home for your children.
D Thanks. They love balloons.

Page 128, Exercise 2 – Track 35
Graduation Party Gifts
I had a graduation party last Friday. My husband sent invitations to my teacher and to my relatives and friends. They all came to the party! Some guests brought gifts for me. My teacher Mrs. Campbell gave me a card. My Aunt Ana brought me flowers. My friend Sue gave me some perfume. My classmate Ruth brought me some cookies. After the party, I wrote them thank-you notes. Tomorrow, I'm going to mail the thank-you notes at the post office.

Page 129, Exercise 4A – Track 36
1. Thanksgiving
2. Independence Day
3. a wedding
4. a housewarming
5. New Year's Eve
6. Mother's Day
7. Halloween
8. a baby shower
9. Valentine's Day

Illustration credits

Kenneth Batelman: 17, 29, 86, 87, 88, 119, 121

Travis Foster: 48 (t,c), 49 (b)

Chuck Gonzales: 9, 13, 43, 46, 47, 52, 72, 95, 107, 124, 133

Brad Hamann: 11, 21, 25, 35, 89, 112

Ted Hammond: 91

Stuart Holmes: 69 (b)

Images courtesy of Precision Dynamics-St. John: 49 (tr)

Jim Kopp: 51, 77, 103 (#1-7), 117, 129

Q2A Media Services: 2, 48 (b), 69 (t), 103 (#8, #9), 129 (#4)

Monika Roe: 36, 37, 62, 75, 113, 127

Lucy Truman: 101

Photography credits

Cover front (tl) Andrew Zarivny/Shutterstock, (tr) Stuart Monk/Shutterstock, (r) Gary D Ercole/Photolibrary/Getty Images, (cr) Sam Kolich, (br) Nathan Maxfield/iStockphoto, (c) Monkey Business Images/Shutterstock, (bl) Alistair Forrester Shankie/iStockphoto, (cl) ML Harris/Iconica/Getty Images, (l) Mark Lewis/Digital Vision/Getty Images, back (tc) cloki/Shutterstock, (br) gualtiero boffi/Shutterstock, **4** (r) ©istockphoto/Aldo Murillo, **14** (cl) ©Rob Marmion/Shutterstock, **23** (tl) ©corbisrffancy/Fotolia, (tc) ©John Kroetch/Shutterstock, (tr) ©Raisman/Shutterstock, (bl) ©Stockbyte/Thinkstock, (bc) ©Gary Roebuck/Alamy, (br) ©Getty Images/Thinkstock, **34** (br) ©Comstock/Thinkstock, **39** (tl) ©George Doyle/Thinkstock, (tc) ©Ben Molyneux People/Alamy, (tr) ©Bernhard Classen/Alamy, (cl) ©Monkey Business Images/Shutterstock, (c) ©Paul Bradbury/Alamy, (cr) ©Pressmaster/Shutterstock, (bl) ©nyul/iStockphoto, (bc) ©Niko Guido/iStockphoto, (br) ©Plush Studios/iStockphoto, **49** (tl) ©Steve Debenport /iStockphoto, **63** (tl) ©iofoto/Shutterstock, (tcl) ©iStockphoto/Thinkstock, **65** (tl) ©T.M.O.Pictures/Alamy, (tc) ©VStock/Alamy, (tr) ©Fuse/Getty Images, (cl) ©LMR Group/Alamy, (c) ©Veronika Surovtseva/iStockphoto, (cr) ©ParkerDeen/iStockphoto, (bl) ©oliveromg/Shutterstock, (bc) ©Krzysztof Kwiatkowski/iStockphoto, (br) ©i love images/city break/Alamy, **66** (t) ©rabbit75_fot/Fotolia, (b) ©JLImages/Alamy, **73** (tl) ©ruchos/Shutterstock, (tcl) ©artemisphoto/Fotolia, **74** (cr) ©diego cervo/Fotolia, **78** (cr) ©OtnaYdur/Shutterstock, **92** (tl) ©digitaldarrell/Shutterstock, (tc) ©iStockphoto/Thinkstock, (tr) ©MaxxStudio/Shutterstock, **93** (tr) ©iStockphoto/Thinkstock, **98** (r) ©Monkey Business/Fotolia, **125** (tl) ©Renewer/Shutterstock, (tc) ©Stocksnapper/Shutterstock, (tr) ©Marjanneke de Jong/Shutterstock, (cl) ©Erena.Wilson/Shutterstock, (c) ©Yasonya/Fotolia, (cr) ©marco mayer/Shutterstock, (bl) ©TigerForce/Shutterstock, (bc) ©Brenda Carson/Fotolia, (br) ©Gresei/Fotolia

Track (STUDENT TK) Listing for Self-Study Audio CD

Track	Page	Exercise
1		
2	3	2A
3	4	3A
4	4	3B
5	5	4A
6	5	4B
7	7	2A and 2B
8	12	2
9	13	4A
10	19	2A and 2B
11	24	2
12	25	4A

Track	Page	Exercise
13	33	2A and 2B
14	38	2
15	39	4A
16	45	2A and 2B
17	50	2
18	51	4A
19	59	2A and 2B
20	64	2
21	65	4A
22	71	2A and 2B
23	76	2
24	77	4A

Track	Page	Exercise
25	85	2A and 2B
26	90	2
27	91	4A
28	97	2A and 2B
29	102	2
30	103	4A
31	111	2A and 2B
32	116	2
33	117	4A
34	123	2A and 2B
35	128	2
36	129	4A